BUSINESS

and the

BEAUTIFUL
GAME

Praise for *Business and the Beautiful Game*

"I am indebted to the authors for writing this book. I now feel fully justified in my habit of peppering my management talks with sporting analogies. Just when I was beginning to think I'd overdone it, I now find countless examples in here, and I can't wait to introduce them into my talks, oblivious to the pleading looks from my audience. In sport, you see competition in its purest form. There's no grey, no amount of management speak can gloss over the result. There are lots of lessons, I believe, for managers to see what really matters when the pressure is on."

Sir Terry Leahy, CEO, Tesco

"In any profession you've got to have passion... the more desire you have the better the chance you've got of reaching the top."

Bryan Robson, former Captain, England

"Theobald and Cooper confirm what many people have suspected for some time – leadership and management in football and business are variations on the same theme. Very readable and relevant for all those interested in business management."

Alan Murray, CEO, Hanson PLC

"Competition, strategy and tactics, leadership, management and teamwork are all carefully analysed. The book is striking and evocative. It will appeal to all practitioners and students of commerce, especially those with a love for the beautiful game."

Keith Harris, former Chairman, the Football League

"What a great read! This will inspire not only those in business but in sport too. Want to motivate your staff? Give them a copy today!"

Martin Edwards, former Chairman, Manchester United FC

"The use of business practice in the world of soccer is both innovative and exciting. This book provides the insight and is a great read!"

Keith Edelman, Managing Director, Arsenal FC

BUSINESS
and the
BEAUTIFUL
GAME

**HOW YOU CAN APPLY THE SKILLS & PASSION
OF FOOTBALL TO BE A WINNER IN BUSINESS**

Theo Theobald & Cary Cooper

KOGAN
PAGE

For Hazel

Whose selfless dedication to Alan led her to Tranmere Rovers on many a freezing Friday night.

Theo Theobold

I would like to thank Sir Roland and Lady Joan Smith for igniting my passion in the beautiful game, and to my club Manchester City FC for a wonderful roller coaster ride all these years!

Cary Cooper

Publisher's note
Every possible effort has been made to ensure that the information contained in this book is accurate at the time of going to press, and the publishers and authors cannot accept responsibility for any errors or omissions, however caused. No responsibility for loss or damage occasioned to any person acting, or refraining from action, as a result of the material in this publication can be accepted by the editor, the publisher or any of the authors.

First published in Great Britain in 2005 by Kogan Page Limited

120 Pentonville Road
London N1 9JN
United Kingdom
www.kogan-page.co.uk

ISBN 0 7494 4354 5

British Library Cataloguing-in-Publication Data

A CIP record for this book is available from the British Library.

Typeset by Saxon Graphics Ltd, Derby
Printed and bound in Great Britain by Creative Print and Design (Wales), Ebbw Vale

Contents

The Second Half

About the authors

Theo Theobald is an established author of business and lifestyle books, and his varied career in marketing and advertising includes management positions with the BBC and creative roles within the independent sector. His creative writing career has involved major internet and audio production for such companies as the BBC and the CIPD. In 2001 he started his own company, Shocktactic Ltd, and he is also a renowned public speaker.

Cary L Cooper is Professor of Organizational Psychology and Health at Lancaster University and President of the British Academy of Management. The author of over 100 books on management, he writes regularly for the national and specialist press and is a frequent guest on radio and television, where his views are sought on a range of business issues and on life in general.

Pre-match preparation

'Before you set foot on the pitch, find out more about what you're letting yourself in for.'

This isn't the traditional preface that you might expect to find at the front of any other business book; we've dropped that in favour of a football analogy, because that's what this is about, taking what we know about our 'beautiful game' and transferring the learning into the workplace at every level from top floor to shop floor.

It's not a book about the business side of the game of football, because that, as they say, is a whole new can of worms; however, what you will find is insight into how football works and the relevance of its component parts for those of us in less glamorous (but probably more secure) jobs.

Our first advice is 'don't forget to warm up properly' and, with that in mind, this short introduction, or pre-match pep talk, is designed to help you get the best out of the following pages, by outlining what to expect when you 'get on the pitch'.

There are chapters on EMOTIONAL elements, like passion and ambition – you'd expect nothing less when talking about Britain's national sport – and there are others on ANALYTICAL features of football, like coaching and teamwork, which play just as vital a role.

It seemed logical and potentially most beneficial to focus part of the book on you as an individual, and all of that comes in the section we've called the 'first half' (you see we really are staying true to the football analogy). During this voyage of self-discovery, you can test yourself to find out 'how ambitious you are' and why it matters; later you'll have the opportunity to determine your personal level of self-discipline and understand the effect it has on people close to you. We talk about the good things like self-belief and how to assess and improve your skills; as well as all that, we look at some of the obstacles you'll need to overcome if you are to be truly successful, including a whole section on stress and how to cope with it.

After half time (in the 'second half') we turn our attention to tactics, with an examination of 'coaching', 'team selection' and 'coping with the opposition', and provide an analysis of some of the key roles like 'manager' and 'captain', which you might already be occupying, or hope to soon.

Imagine that reading the book is like watching the match on Sky Interactive; you can do it your own way. You may decide to sit through the whole game from beginning to end (reading in a linear way from cover to cover), or alternatively, just the highlights might suit you better, in which case a quick dip in and out will satisfy your hunger. If you choose the latter route, it's better if you select a full chapter, as a page or two out of context is much less beneficial (it's like seeing the goal scored without knowing what the build-up was).

There are many examples that we give in the text which can apply to one discipline or the other (football or business), and where the link is glaringly obvious we've tried to resist the urge to patronize you by pointing it out, so in some instances we talk in football terms, in others, business. Where it's more difficult to see the linkage, we go into more depth to show the similarity between the two subjects.

We haven't made any attempt to avoid some of the better-known footballing clichés and make no apologies for that – it was just too tempting – but beyond the 'sick as a parrot' and the 'game of two halves', there's plenty of more thoughtful input, not only from us as the authors, but from a fantastic line-up of people from the world of football and business whose wisdom we uncovered as a result of our research. Our thanks go to all who contributed their time and knowledge, with special gratitude to Fast Web Media for their help in obtaining many relevant quotations from football personalities.

Even if you've been in business for only a relatively short period of time, some of the text will be familiar to you, especially elements like working as part of a team, but if, like us, you've been around a bit longer, there are some revelations about how football works which we can all learn from. You'll find everything from 'poaching to coaching', from 'tactical to practical'.

Most of all, we hope we've provided a framework for a fresh way of thinking about business and a set of metaphors for helping remember what's important both on and off the pitch.

Come on then, get those boots laced up, it's time for kick-off.

Features of the book

Yes, we know you're gagging to get out there, but before you do, here is a bit of advance information on what you'll find; it may help you understand the game you're playing a bit better.

Sound Bite

When you see this picture, it represents a sound bite. Media is increasingly influential in the world of football and ever more intrusive; how far away are we from the day when the TV cameras will be allowed in the dressing room at half time? It's only fair to point out that this is a bit of a reciprocal arrangement, as the 'beautiful game' would not have grown to its current popularity (and subsequent ability to generate cash) had it not been for the increase in media exposure. There's an early lesson for business managers too; the outside world can increasingly see inside your organization to the kind of 'below stairs' stuff you used to like to keep hidden. The internet is partly responsible for this, but so too is our modern attitude, which no longer treats the 'secrets' of an organization with the reverence of old. All this media growth has produced a tendency to sum situations up in a short sound bite, so we've decided to start each chapter with one as a kind of shorthand comment on what you can expect.

On the Ball

This icon symbolizes a feature we've called 'on the ball'; it's a collection of stories that help to illustrate a particular element of the text. Some are true, others are based on what really happened (with the names changed to save us being sued) and the remainder are overheard anecdotes or pure fiction; we think they're all equally valid in being able to bring a particular point to life.

Tactics

At the end of each chapter you'll find this icon, which is the start of the chapter summary. In each case we've tried to pick out half a dozen or so of the major learning points and have called the section 'tactics' because it is what we *do* that makes businesses work, not what we think about, say or debate with our colleagues. For that reason we've tried to make sure the 'tactics' give practical tips on how to conduct yourself.

Pundit

This symbolizes the views of experts. Sometimes these are one-liners and at others full stories from pundits who have followed the game or been involved in it for most of their lives. It is their insight which has helped form our opinions and support our theories.

Training Tip

Short bursts of additional learning, or ways of changing your thinking and your actions are incorporated in a collection of training tips throughout the text. You'll find that these are marked out by this symbol.

Now, is that the roar of the crowd we can hear...?

The First Half

1

Skills

'You can teach a turkey to climb a tree, but it's better to hire a monkey.'

This chapter on skills puts the focus very much on you as an individual, giving you the chance to have a good hard look at what you're good at and how to exploit it. We also encourage you to think about when it is appropriate to put time and effort into increasing the skills of the team you manage, and when it is better to face up to the fact that a new injection of talent is needed.

The value of skills in the war for talent

You need only to look at escalating transfer costs and the weekly wages of Premiership players to appreciate how 'valuable' skills are to football clubs. The first thing that top players do for a club is help them to win games, and as the margin between winners and losers gets ever closer, one individual in any part of the field can make the difference.

The second thing that clubs expect from their talent is that they will continue to draw crowds in week after week, increasing the immediate revenue of the club. The addition of a new star player can add value for season ticket holders and significantly boost merchandising revenues.

Take this analogy into the business arena and we can start to understand how any one person can influence both the task in hand and the morale of those around them; and in businesses which operate in competitive environments, it's equally true to say that individual effort can affect a much bigger picture.

What is your value?

Working out exactly what you're worth is difficult, no matter what you do for a living, but understanding your 'own value' is half the battle in achieving your ambitions. Often from the outside it's much easier to be objective and understand the value of an individual, so it helps if you operate in a supportive peer group where openness and honesty are part of the currency. Mutual appreciation societies full of talentless 'no hopers' fall outside this category.

In football, a third party with a vested interest plays a big part; we're talking about agents, whose job it is to hype up the value of their players to the highest possible level, by fair means, or sometimes, foul.

The laws of economics dictate that the value of ANYTHING is the price that someone is willing to pay, so a bottle of mineral water at a top London hotel might fetch four or five times the amount it would in a supermarket. Mostly we're prepared to pay up because of the surroundings we're in and the 'added value' that they provide. Value here is not about the cost of the water, but the atmosphere, the experience, and more, right down to the linen tablecloth and the immaculately attired (and fawning) waiter.

So what is the correlation between the amount a football club is willing to pay for a top international 'star' and your own value in the world of work that you've chosen?

The first thing to remember is that your value will be broken in two by any prospective 'buyer'. They'll look first at what you can achieve for them now and then at what your future potential is.

Personnel managers and scouts look at the world in the same way; each of them is trying to match up the skills of the individual with the skill gap of the organization. So a team that's letting in too many goals might be looking for a solid central defender; a company that's losing market share to competitors will be seeking a skilled marketing expert. Before you even start to consider your worth, you need to work out if you're filling an essential gap and what your particular skill mix will add to the team/company.

The final thing to say about value is that for all this analysis, it is often still a subjective thing and because of this it's usually true that your 'starting value' will define or limit the amount you can aspire to. Let's say you join a company on a salary of £20K per annum; it's unlikely that however much you achieve they will double your salary. However, if you apply for a job with a competitor for £40K, and they think your skills match their skill gap sufficiently, you may well make the leap. Only then will your original company be able to think of you as a £40K contender. The longer you stay 'typecast' as a £20K-a-year merchant, the harder it will be to convince anyone that you're worth more.

We all have to start somewhere and we heard recently about a £120 payment to one of the country's most successful boy bands for a personal appearance early in their careers; at the height of their fame they were probably earning the same amount per second – they were still the same human beings, but their perceived value had increased, so they could demand more.

Training Tip

Self-discovery

Most of the time, when we're asked what we're good at, we tend to talk about work-based achievements, and while this forms some of the picture, it goes only a small part of the way to describing *us* as individuals. In this exercise you have the opportunity to look at yourself in a more rounded way.

Head up three columns on a sheet of A4 with Social, Practical and Work, and in each of them take a few minutes to think of five things you're good at. There's no need for modesty here, because you're not being asked to share this information with anyone. If it helps, try to think back to when other people have complimented you; have they described you as witty, sporty, compassionate, clever? All of these things contribute towards your unique skill mix.

With these lists in front of you, consider three important elements of your personality.

1. Practical vs. Cerebral – are you a doer or a thinker? Are you happy to get stuck in and get your hands dirty (both literally and figuratively) or are you more considered in your approach, preferring to use your head to work out a solution?
2. Risk averse vs. Risk taker – think about your attitude to risk in different scenarios; when you bet on the Grand National, do you choose a plucky outsider or the trusted favourite? Do you prefer extreme sports or tiddlywinks? Would you risk your company's money? Your own money?
3. Introvert vs. Extrovert – would you be the first to grab the karaoke microphone? Do you like intimate bars or lively night clubs? Solitaire or Twister?

Think of each of these three things like a sliding scale and don't get too hung up about specifics; simply try to establish a general picture of yourself.

Once you've thought about who you are and what you're good at, you next need to consider how well you match the organization you're in or would like to be in. Who are the people working there at the moment, how would you typify their characters and what is it they're trying to achieve? Think, as well, about their attitude to risk; are they thinkers or doers, introverts or extroverts?

Take these two examples:

1. If you're introverted, self-aware and compassionate, with a social conscience and a dislike of injustice, you might choose a more vocational career, perhaps in the public sector or with a not-for-profit organization like a charity.
2. If you're outgoing, gregarious, self-motivated and driven, a better option might be a sales career or a challenging people-management role.

The essential skill mix

From youth level through to professional status, there are three things that define skills in football: the technical, the tactical and the practical. We'll outline these elements in more detail here, but while you're reading, think about how they can be applied to management techniques in your business.

Technical describes the nuts and bolts of how you play the game; it's simply about how well you can do the things that contribute to being a great player. This will vary a bit according to the position you play, but will include things like ball control, dribbling, passing, tackling and heading,

Tactical is far more about the level of awareness you have for what is going on around you. What are your teammates doing, where are they positioned, how are the opposition playing the game, where are they strong in comparison to you, what's happening off the ball?

And finally, the *practical* covers all the other elements that will contribute to you playing at your very best, like fitness, strength, stamina and recovery rate, both from playing and from injury.

Business management is identical to this inasmuch as you need to understand where your strengths are, you need to play to them to maximize your effectiveness, but you also need to be aware of the 'game' that's going on around you, both in your own team and in that of the competitors, or opposition. Finally, if you're not in the best possible shape, and in business this means mentally, physically and emotionally, then you won't maximize your potential.

Six critical skills

So what are the skills you'll need for the future and what can business learn from football in this regard? We've listed six things from the world of football which we believe are essential to the success of any business manager.

1. Control

On the field of play this means ball control, but it could also be interpreted as self-control. Business managers certainly need lots of that, in order to be able to discipline themselves to make the most of the finite time in any working day.

Being in control only comes about through careful planning, which involves allocating a priority to tasks, fixing a timescale by which they will be achieved and knowing what resources are available to help complete them.

Planning also means you'll know what you're going to say to whom and when in order to keep the business running in the most efficient way. Although there is a time and a place for spontaneity, it's hard to imagine that a football manager would deliver his half-time team talk completely off the cuff; it's much more likely that there will be a prepared outline for the message, which he can adapt according to how the first half has gone.

Time and effort put into the preparation phase allows business managers the luxury of staying in control, of themselves and their work/life balance, of situations that are likely to arise (with contingency plans already formulated) and of other members of the team.

Many people shy away from the idea of controlling others, but it's nothing to be afraid of if it's handled correctly and for the greater good of the team as a whole. You're not so much taking control of their personality as shaping their behaviour.

If you've ever witnessed a gang of really small children play football, they run around like a herd of sheep, following the ball which is in the middle of the pack. Someone has to take control of that situation if any of the children are to develop into well-rounded players. Influencing behaviour so that they understand about positional play and the importance of remaining in their allocated role is control in a sense, but everyone benefits.

The same positive outcomes can result in business, if, as a manager, you are able to be clear about roles and stay in control of the situation.

2. Touch

This is an interesting skill because it's quite hard to define, but you'll often hear football pundits describing a player as having 'great touch'.

Partly it's to do with judgement – judgement of many things, including what's happening in the wider picture, but also of the pace of the ball, the state of the pitch, the atmosphere of the game and the mood and morale of other players.

There's a great degree of subtlety to 'touch' and it's easy to see how in a business context this can be translated into situations that might be regarded as 'moments of truth', like the delicate stages of a negotiation or a particularly difficult performance management interview.

The commercial interpretation of 'touch' would also include a need to be adaptable in your game plan, judging what *feelings* are around and making small adjustments to cater for them.

3. Vision

Vision has got itself a bit of a bad name over recent years, partly because it has become inextricably linked with that most useless of business tools, the mission statement. We say this not because we don't see the worth of collecting everyone around a single idea, but because most mission statements are so wordy and unfocused that not only do staff not know them, but they don't know what they mean either. If you're looking for an antidote to mission-statement madness then take a leaf out of the Lexus car manufacturer's book, whose simple mantra was only two words, 'Beat Mercedes!'

Of course it's important to know where you're headed, but the rigid framework of these statements often is far from being all-inclusive.

In football there is a pretty clear vision, to win as many points and trophies as possible, but in business there may be many conflicting priorities. Certainly the organization as a whole needs a target, aim, objective or goal, but it is likely that this will translate into a very diverse set of tasks per individual manager and worker.

One of the interpretations of vision that is often neglected in business is that of the 'visionary individual', for this is someone who through experience can anticipate what's going to happen next. An 'attacking midfielder' will be able to spot an opportunity to overturn an offside trap and play the ball into the path of a striker, whose forward run he's anticipated.

Very often in business there is a lack of this kind of foresight, and it's only by staying awake to what's happening in the organization and the wider world that you can hope to acquire and develop this most valuable of skills.

4. Awareness

Self-awareness is a critical element of success, and hopefully some of the analysis techniques that we recommend will help you with that. It's only when we understand about our strengths and weaknesses and take some steps to address that situation that we can make the most of our potential.

But understanding oneself is not enough. There is also the need to look up and see what is happening around you; on the pitch this will help your anticipation skills, but it will also allow you to see the things that are working well for you and the areas where you are subject to 'attack'.

Exactly the same applies in a commercial setting, although seeing what is about to happen and taking action to maximize the opportunity is never easy. This is in part due to the fact that many managers suffer from work overload and don't have the time to look up and around. Large organizations also tend to suffer from what's become known as 'silo mentality', where one department works in isolation (in its own silo), not connected to any other; the result is that the HR department don't know what the marketing team are doing and operational staff and management are so busy trying to maximize their own productivity that they have little connection with the sales force.

Under circumstances like these it's easy to see how your improved anticipation skills could become extremely valuable.

Training Tip

A picture of you

We felt the need to add a final footnote on the specific subject of self-awareness. You can come to a fairly accurate picture of the person you are through a host of different channels. What do friends say about you? What do you love and hate doing (which is a good indicator of what you're good and bad at), what self-assessment exercises can you take (both in this book and elsewhere)? What does your boss say about you at appraisal time?

Gather together the collective learning from all these sources and you're left with a pretty accurate picture of yourself. With a list of your strengths and weaknesses in front of you, there are two schools of thought on what to do next. The first says you must put time and effort into addressing the things you're bad at, as it is these very weaknesses that will drag you down and stop you from reaching your full potential.

Our view is different. Yes, you need to be aware of the things you're not so good at, and even put a limited amount of time, effort and resources into making some improvement, but most of your attention should be devoted to what you already excel at. *Make people recognize you for the positive things you bring to the business, but be self-effacing enough to recognize the things that you like less.*

A good example would be if you were a creative 'ideas' person but had a short attention span and hated detail; if this is you, then play to that strength and try to make sure there are people around you in the organization who can pick up your ideas and see them through and someone else to tidy up the loose ends along the way; you can then be left to get on with what you're really good at, rather than stifling the creation of new ideas by getting bogged down in the detail.

5. Resilience

So just how tough are you? If you go 1–0 down, will the whole game plan collapse, will the team lose its shape and its discipline? Will everyone start to panic?

Being able to bounce back in the face of adversity is something we tend to learn with experience. The first time we encounter a crisis at work we may run around like a headless chicken, but once we learn (the hard way) that this does nothing to solve the problem, we're more likely to find a way of moving forward which involves keeping a cool head and making the best out of what is a bad situation.

Lots more organizations are realizing the benefits of allowing their people to make mistakes (but not if they repeat them), as this is key to learning the right way to do things. In that kind of environment there needs to be plenty of support to allow individuals to build up their own resilience and then to help others develop the same skill.

6. Fitness

We touched earlier on the fact that business managers have to keep themselves in good shape if they're going to be effective.

Certainly fitness is a key element on the field of play; speed and stamina can help players to avoid injury, but even if it does occur, recovery is much quicker if you're in good physical condition to start with.

Physical fitness is important for all of us though, especially if we're going to operate at maximum efficiency. Too many cigarettes, too much alcohol, a poor diet and lack of exercise result in business managers whose mental capacity is reduced: their decision making gets poorer and their stress levels increase; certainly they are less able to cope in a crisis.

The good news is that of all the skills we've talked about, fitness is the one we can most easily influence ourselves.

Finally, we'd like to stretch a point on fitness and think about it in terms of being 'fit for purpose'. It really is worth thinking about how well suited you are to your current role; knowing how well your existing skills match your job description is a skill in itself and it's one that can influence us to make important career change decisions.

On the Ball

The relevance of skills

To finish this section about the skills needed to make effective business managers we pick up on the last point about 'fit for purpose' skills.

A large media organization introduced a 360 degree appraisal system into its most cynical management team, which involved all managers helping in the performance management of each other.

Each sent the others a questionnaire that listed five key competencies of managers and asked the respondent to mark, out of 10, how important these were to the job title of the manager in question; it then went on to ask for a mark out of 10 on the basis of how skilled that individual was in applying them.

For example, 'the ability to prioritize and execute a planned framework of activity for each member of your team'; this may score 8 out of 10 for relevance to the role and you might score 7 out of 10 for your ability to do it.

After a few weeks of completing feedback forms, one manager commented that whenever he had to fill them in for a colleague, he put 10 out of 10 for the first section and 0 out of 10 for the second, meaning that these were all critical elements of the job, but the manager was useless at carrying them out.

'I do it the other way round', replied his colleague, 'which gives the result that none of these things matters a damn to their particular role, but my word are they good at them?!'

The serious point to the story is that the wrong person in the wrong role results in poor performance; we can apply that to our own role, or look at it in the light of the people we are managing, but either way it indicates a mismatch. In a situation like this, it's more likely that the individual will be better served by moving on than by a comprehensive retraining programme, but you need to be clear in advance where the round pegs and the round holes are!

Light at the end of the tunnel

Mostly in this chapter we've talked about a generic set of skills that are as important in the boardroom as on the training ground. But all of this thinking has been around a set of personal attributes, and there are many other 'micro-skills' you'll need in order to be able to perform your day job.

You'll normally find a list of these in a job advertisement, for example 'experience of PowerPoint and Word', or 'ability to handle complex data and draw swift conclusions', and the good news about most of these things is that they can be learnt over time.

With a greater awareness of your strengths and weaknesses you can start to plug some of the gaps that you think are important to your future development, by reading up on a subject, returning to college or negotiating some on-the-job training with your existing employer. As we said earlier, *play to your strengths if you want to make the most of the skill mix you possess.*

More enlightened HR

We've highlighted above the traditional way of recruiting, which has been employed by HR departments for many years. A list of required skills will often sort the wheat from the chaff at an early stage of the recruitment process. However, it has been recognized more and more in recent times that in many sectors, particularly with customer-facing roles or in service industries, what people can do right now is less important than how they might approach it.

The new thinking in these circumstances states that organizations need to recruit for ATTITUDE and train for SKILL.

It's based on the fact that you can take people with the right mindset and train them to do the task in hand; however, if you've got people already competent but with bad attitude, you'll never realize the potential of the organization.

Tactics

■ All businesses and football clubs are searching for skills to enhance their team.

■ Understanding your own skills helps you assess what you're 'worth'.

■ Your starting 'value' usually determines what people believe you are worth.

■ When you know yourself you are better able to find a role you'll be happy in.

■ Important skills include the technical, tactical and practical.

■ Control, touch, vision, awareness, resilience and fitness are six essential skills.

The easiest team for a manager to pick is the Hindsight XI. (Craig Brown – ex-Scotland manager)

2

Ambition

Sound Bite

'In the engine room of achievement, it's ambition that fuels the fire.'

There are lots of words and phrases we can use to sum up ambition, like 'hunger', 'will to win' and 'desire'.

Although, like passion (which forms a separate chapter), this is an emotive area, it differs in as much as our level of control over ambition is much greater, many things change our view of what we want to achieve and the ambitions that burn in us may change as we progress through our careers. But ambition can be dangerous too, if it's not harnessed by reality. If our desire burns too strongly, if we simply want to achieve our goal too much, it can blight our lives. In the end, if we can't achieve our ambition by fair means, then we may readily turn to foul.

That's a very apt phrase when applied to the football field, as one player attempts to 'clatter' another, either to interrupt that particular play or to ensure that in subsequent encounters he'll have the upper hand.

To openly accuse an opponent of 'cheating' is beyond the pale in the media-facing part of the game, but behind the scenes, on the terraces and in the pubs during post-match analysis, you'll hear the term coined again and again.

'Diving in the box', attempting to have opposition players sent off and complaining needlessly to the referee in an effort to sway his decisions are all forms of cheating that are rife. Below this level, there's another layer that's hard to define; some would call it cheating, some 'gamesmanship'.

On the Ball

Sunday League

Many Sunday League players will be familiar with the scenario of 'claiming' for everything; it's actively encouraged. When the ball goes out of play, there's a certain type of character who will always turn to the referee with a shout of 'our ball'. This occurs when the most blatant evidence is against them, even when the ball has quite clearly come off one of their own players, 'Ref, our ball!' goes up the shout.

The behaviour they adopt is built on the premise that all human beings make wrong decisions sometimes and that by continually questioning the referee, the culprits of this practice seek to undermine both his authority and his confidence, and from time to time have an outcome in their favour that they do not deserve.

This mentality seems to be more rife in football than in other sports; it's certainly not something you see on the rugby pitch, and an equivalent in cricketing terms would be to shout 'Owzat' after every ball, which seems a bit implausible.

Is this cheating though, or just a bit of gamesmanship? Is it simply part of the rough and tumble of the game, or does it signal the tip of an ill-intentioned and malicious iceberg? Even in the professional game we see instances where one player will feign injury after a tackle, in order to get the perpetrator sent off; officially this is known as 'bringing the game into disrepute', unofficially it's called 'being a sneaky b*****d!'.

On the Ball

Unbridled fair-mindedness

So that you don't get the impression that all footballers are cheats who seek to do down the opposition in any way they can, we include this story to warm the cockles of your heart.

There is an unwritten rule in football that if the game is halted because a player is injured, upon the restart, possession of the ball is gifted back to the side whose player needed treatment. In a Carling Cup tie between Yeovil and Plymouth, a bizarre goal was scored when the Yeovil striker,

Lee Johnson, attempted to pass the ball back to the Plymouth keeper after just such an injury stoppage. However, he failed to notice that the keeper was off his line and the ball rolled over, leaving the referee with no option but to award the goal. In the spirit of fairness, the Yeovil manager instructed his players to allow Plymouth to cancel out the mistake, by standing still while striker Steve Crawford walked casually through the lot of them and scored unopposed.

Many of us have been brought up on the adage that 'cheats never prosper', which in our experience is quite clearly abject nonsense. I'd be surprised if any of us can't think of an individual or a scenario where evil has triumphed over good because of the intervention of a bit of well-timed cheating, but that doesn't make it right or for that matter sustainable in the longer term.

We've seen what this ambition-driven cheating looks like on the football field, but what about the workplace? At the Sunday League level it might include a bit of bending of the truth to try to make yourself appear better, perhaps by undermining those around you. In the business arena, it might involve the 'doing down' of the opposition, that's to say bad-mouthing your competitors in the market or making extravagant (and unprovable) claims about your own product as against theirs.

But, up the ante in this way and soon you could be into dangerous territory; take the questionable principles of the seasoned cheat into the boardroom and soon you'll be looking at pension scheme collapse, insider dealing and the demise of whole corporations, simply because someone had the gas turned up too high when they were cooking the books. All of this has already happened.

And what causes such unreasonable behaviour in intelligent human beings? They may claim it's about personal ambition, but from the outside it looks as though that's spilled over into greed; the one is a small step away from the other.

Personal or cultural?

I bet you can think of someone right now whose drive and will to win make you feel uncomfortable inside. When someone is more ambitious than us we find it hard to fathom out; what factors in their past have made them burn inside in this way?

But outside the analysis of individuals comes the cultural and social factors that can make a whole nation more ambitious than another or a particular time in history that encourages selfishness over selflessness. American business icon Donald Trump is known for his uncompromising attitude to business life and his advice includes: never quit, think big, be paranoid, go against the tide and, most importantly of all, always get a prenuptial agreement! Here are a few more collected Americanisms that some feel typify their cultural attitude to business:

- Winners never quit – quitters never win.
- America – love it or leave it!
- Keep your friends close and your enemies closer.
- Don't get mad, get even.
- My country – right or wrong!

On the Ball

Open and honest

As further evidence of the importance of national culture, here is a transcript of a real conversation that took place in the lobby of a Dallas hotel which was hosting a major conference; it was between two American businessmen who'd met only once before:

Man 1 (shouting across the lobby): Say Bob! Bob how are ya doin'?
Man 2 (clearly nonplussed): Err I'm fine, have we met?
Man 1: Sure, I saw you lecture at this conference two years ago and we had a chat afterwards… I'm Brad, Brad Boulter…
Man 2 (uncertainly): Oh, sure yes, Brad, well tell me Brad, what happened to you?
Man 1 (delivered without a flicker): Oh, *I got successful!*

This is how up front you're allowed to be in the United States and if that mindset is commonplace it's easy to see how ambition will not only thrive but will be considered the norm. It doesn't mean that the Americans are wrong in how they act; they're simply conforming to the norms of their own culture.

True Brit

It's a terribly British thing *not* to celebrate success; some would say it explains the nation's relatively poor showing on the world stage of sport (and probably other things too), but most Brits were brought up to 'hide their light under a bushel', and look slightly abashed if anyone else should notice it.

It may seem astounding to other nationalities but there's a general feeling in Britain that we'd rather be plucky losers than boastful winners. Of course when success does come along, we can dance in the streets with the best of them; it's just that the next morning we feel a little embarrassed at having done so.

This contrast of national psyche is designed to show how behaviour can change according to the environment we're operating in. We've used national boundaries to illustrate this, as it's easier to grasp the concept that way, but sometimes the environment we're in is created by the people who are in it now and the history of the place. In that way, football clubs can create their own micro-environment and, having set the culture, the impact is far reaching, including attitudes to ambition.

As we've hinted, ambition can be of its time too; despite the usual reserve of the British, the 1980s turned normally mild-mannered considerate individuals into corporate rottweilers – it was the age of the me-society.

On the Ball

Chuck's story

Sometimes the will to win can end up causing irreparable damage; pain-killing injections are a part of the professional game, but even at a lower level, people are prepared to go to extremes in an effort to come out on top.

Chuck is an 18-stone Canadian hulk with massive upper body strength and knees so badly damaged that he has to wear leg braces for even the gentlest exercise. At 27 he has some regrets about his former will to win:

When I was 16, I was desperate to keep my place in the [American] football team at high school; I needed some kind of track record to take with me to college, especially if I was going to make it at that level.

I started taking steroids then and soon found out that most of the rest of the guys on my team were; without them you simply couldn't compete. None of us were ever going to make it even into the lowest level of the professional game but we felt the need to try; we'd swallowed the dream, along with the pills. I got stronger on the drugs, but so did the other guys and boy did I take a pounding; now I look back and wonder why we bothered; my knees are shot to pieces and there's no going back.

The life cycle of ambition

In football, in business and in life our ambitions change as we get older. This is nature's way of preventing us from becoming too disappointed with our achievements. Clearly, the physical clock is ticking for all of us and this is an horrific prospect for professional footballers. When we're young it's of little concern (and rightly so, we'll have plenty of time to worry about it later), but it does mean that we tend to aim high.

Partly this is driven by the 'innocence of youth', and while older and more cynical people may be trying to pull them back down to earth with their goal setting, it is exactly this kind of exuberance that helps each successive generation to achieve to its potential.

What we're saying is that you should never be put off by managers (in football or business) who attempt to stifle your enthusiasm. If they are truly wise they'll counsel you about how to put milestones in place to show your achievement and what to do when things don't work out as expected. As Mark Twain once suggested, 'keep away from people who try to belittle your ambitions. Small people always do that, but the really great people make you feel that you too can somehow become great.'

On the Ball

A bit too ambitious

When it comes to being ambitious about the future, there is no one more optimistic than Mohamed Al Fayed, the Harrods owner and millionaire businessman behind Fulham FC. When he took control of the club in 1997 they were in the Second Division and such was Mr Al Fayed's level of ambition that he said in a radio interview that he believed the club could make it to the Premiership next season. This was a physical impossibility as they would need to spend at least a year in the First Division before stepping up to the top flight.

We'll look at planning for the future in more detail during the second half, but for now it's worth bearing in mind that goals are better broken down into stages, each with its own anticipated time frame; some contingency planning also needs to be built into the system to allow for unforeseen events, like an injury or a commercial setback.

Training Tip

A way of thinking about ambition (with apologies to Maslow)

One of the most frequently talked about models of management theory is Maslow's hierarchy of needs. Developed by Abraham Maslow of New York in the 1940s and 50s it describes what motivates us and where each of us sets our ambitions. Although it's been mucked about a fair amount since then, mostly by so-called gurus trying to bask in Maslow's reflected glory, the theory remains pretty much the same.

Briefly it goes like this: Maslow drew a pyramid and sliced it horizontally into a number of sections (Figure 2.1). At the broad base of the pyramid he included man's most basic needs of food and shelter, the things we all require just to stay alive. Rising through each section there are a range of other desirable things we'd want to have in our lives; once we'd satisfied the needs lower down, this might include love, affection and a sense of belonging. At the pointy top of the pyramid comes our ultimate ambition of 'self-actualization'; this is when we are at one with the world and at peace with ourselves, all our needs and wants satisfied.

What might this have meant to a young aspiring football professional?

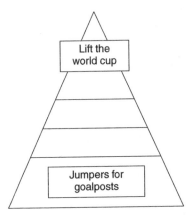

Figure 2.1   If Maslow had been a footie fan

Once you've grasped this analogy you can translate it back into business terms; you can then decide what's your own personal 'jumpers for goalposts' and, more importantly from an ambition point of view, what your World Cup will be represented by.

What are you ambitious for?

Sometimes it really does feel that we have no time to stand and stare. One of the things that afflicts our modern lives is the pace of them, which contributes to us never really stopping to think about what we want. So when we say we're ambitious, just what are we ambitious for? Here are some traditional goals to think about:

■ money
■ fame
■ fortune
■ notoriety
■ power
■ responsibility
■ attention.

The thing about writing them down like that is that they all start to look a bit shallow, so with your own ambitions have a good hard think about what your 'end game' might be. Will you want people to look back on your life and think of you as the most powerful person in your profession, or would it be better if that were tempered with a more caring attitude towards others? Only you can judge.

What most of the things in the list lead to is that many of us are looking for recognition of a job well done; we want people to see that we're good at something and acknowledge that we've used our skills to the best advantage – having lots of money and a big car are just symbols of that, a kind of badge of honour.

Ken Blanchard, author of the *One Minute Manager*, says that lots of people today seem to put too much store on acquiring material things; 'they think that he who dies with the most toys wins, in reality, he who dies with the most toys... dies!' Or as Woody Allen once said, 'I don't want to achieve immortality through my work – I want to achieve it by not dying!'

Not all pursuits in life have to be worthy ones, but it is important in business to remember now and again the real reason you're doing all of this. Put it this way, if you were to ask a footballer to give up either his FA Cup winner's medal or his Ferrari, you'd soon see how little the material wealth he's accrued is worth in comparison to his sporting achievement. For most of us, we simply want to be able to look back and say, 'I was there.'

Measure your AQ

First came IQ to measure how clever you are, then EQ, the amount of emotional intelligence you possess, now we bring you AQ (ambition quotient), so you can find out just how ambitious you really are. This is not meant to be a psychometric measure, just an indication of your ambitiousness.

Below you'll find a selection of questions covering subjects like football and business, plus some real-life scenarios. Answer the questions as honestly as possible, then check your scores at the end to see your 'personal ambition' rating:

1. You play for a Premiership team that has finished consistently mid-table for the last 3 years. Although you are not cash-rich there is great team spirit. At the start of the season, which of these is your target?
   a. happy to end up mid-table but would like a good Cup run;
   b. the League and Cup double; if you don't aim high, you'll never get anywhere;
   c. don't mind where you finish up as long as you're not relegated;
   d. not that bothered about the team as long as I play well and get bought by a bigger club.
2. When you go on a two-week holiday, do you:
   a. just lie by the pool or on the beach, doing little else;
   b. have some rest on the beach or pool but also see some of the sights;
   c. book onto as many of the organized tours you can fit in;
   d. read the 'rough guide' in advance and set off on your own to ensure that you see everything in the area?
3. When on holiday, I tend to:
   a. never let anybody at work know where I am going;
   b. take my mobile on holiday and very occasionally call the office to check on things;
   c. let people at work know where I am, tell them they can call me while on holiday and/or call the office from time to time on holiday to find out what is happening;
   d. use my wireless laptop to log in every day.
4. When in a long, slow queue at a supermarket, I tend to:
   a. wait my turn and chill out by thinking what I'll cook tonight;
   b. get a bit annoyed, still stay in the queue but show displeasure;
   c. get so frustrated that I tend to find a shorter or faster queue and go to it;
   d. complain loudly to anyone who'll listen.

5. Which of the following words or phrases most closely matches your personality?
   a. even tempered;
   b. volatile;
   c. chilled out;
   d. stressed.

6. How would a good friend describe you?
   a. timid;
   b. tenacious;
   c. aggressive;
   d. laid back.

7. A competitor in your field of business has just started a price war; how do you respond?
   a. slash your prices to a level below theirs;
   b. write to all your customers telling them that your own product is of better quality;
   c. write to all their customers telling them that they've only managed to reduce the price by compromising on quality;
   d. ignore them and get on with your own business.

8. You are being interviewed for a promotion along with one other candidate who is a peer in your organization. Beforehand do you:
   a. wish him or her luck, saying may the best 'man' win;
   b. ignore him or her completely;
   c. act as though you don't care if you get the job or not;
   d. try to undermine his or her confidence in the run-up to the interview?

9. You have just been awarded a new contract from a large client; would you:
   a. just keep it to yourself more or less;
   b. tell a few colleagues (like your boss perhaps) and spouse/friends;
   c. let most of the senior people at work know by e-mailing them or 'dropping it in' at a meeting; or
   d. pin a notice on the board in reception and get IT to set up a banner on the intranet?

10. You are happy in your job and location, but a headhunter calls to ask if you are interested in a more senior job that would involve you moving house; would you:
    a. ask the salary and immediately accept if it's more than you're on;
    b. think it over and discuss it with your spouse/partner;
    c. say you are interested, and then go home and convince your partner about the career opportunities;
    d. say 'thanks anyway but I am content where I am'?

How did you score?

Question 1. a = 2, b = 3, c = 1, d = 4
Question 2. a = 1, b = 2, c = 4, d = 3
Question 3. a = 1, b = 2, c = 4, d = 3
Question 4. a = 1, b = 2, c = 4, d = 3
Question 5. a = 2, b = 3, c = 1, d = 4
Question 6. a = 1, b = 3, c = 4, d = 2
Question 7. a = 4, b = 2, c = 3, d = 1
Question 8. a = 1, b = 3, c = 2, d = 4
Question 9. a = 1, b = 2, c = 3, d = 4
Question 10. a = 4, b = 2, c = 3, d = 1

Having ambition is one thing, achieving it is something else entirely.

What to do with your quiz results

If you scored 10 you are a...

Sloth

Hello! Is there anybody in there? Ambition-wise the lights are on but there's nobody at home.

You are showing the classic signs of someone who's not ambitious. This may not be cause for alarm because it might be down to a number of factors. It could be that you're already pretty content with your lot in life, that you've achieved most of what you want to and that you've calculated that the extra effort to achieve more (whether financial, spiritual or whatever) simply isn't worth it.

There are plenty of people in business who question the reason for their commercial existence, but do nothing about it, so to have got where you want to be is an enviable position. It may be that you now wish to sustain that position, or put your efforts into helping others achieve their goals, in which case you might need to try a bit harder in future.

Another possibility exists and that is that nothing has excited you sufficiently in your working life to make you ambitious. This is sometimes the case in hereditary careers, eg taking over the family firm or following in your father's footsteps and becoming a doctor, despite feeling no real calling.

There's no shame in not being terrifically ambitious; although there are many who believe this might limit your earnings potential, you may be much richer in the long run in terms of quality of life issues.

If you scored between 11 and 20 you are a...

Sheep

You're faster than a sloth, but have a bit of a tendency to follow the pack, when charting your own course would result in greater satisfaction and a higher level of achievement. You need greater incentives than you're currently getting, so refocus your efforts on the things you really want out of life.

On the upside you show yourself to be a real team player and are gratified when the collective effort of you and your peers results in reaching your goal, but every now and again you need to think about being a bit more selfish or you'll spend your life only trying to please others.

If you scored between 21 and 30 you are a...

Tiger

You're tenacious without being tedious. Not only have you set your sights firmly on what you want, but you've gone about getting there in a fair-minded and balanced way.

You're the kind of person who doesn't suffer fools gladly, but at the same time you don't take yourself too seriously either. You're not afraid of hard work, but take care to ensure this doesn't get out of balance with the rest of your life.

Every now and again you'll benefit from taking a break and really thinking hard about where you want to be in 12 months' time; for the sake of your future happiness, make sure you don't restrict your thinking solely to work-based pursuits.

If you scored between 31 and 40 you are a...

Tasmanian Devil

My oh my, we are aggressive aren't we? You wouldn't mind treading on your granny's head to get closer to the top, but it would be better if you could stack the whole family up to get a bit of extra height.

You really are in the 'win-at-all-costs' danger zone, and need to think hard, firstly about what you want to achieve, but more importantly about why. Try to project forward to when you've reached your goal and think what it will feel like; will you really be satisfied?

With this level of energy and determination, you certainly have the potential to go far, but you might find you'll miss out on a lot along the way, not least the relationships that could lead you to be more contented overall. Chill out for a bit; then decide what to do next.

There's no right and wrong with ambition, it's about what suits you as an individual. However, it's such an important part of motivation that you need to make sure you're aiming to achieve your own goal, not someone else's, and it's equally important to have specific milestones, so that you'll know when you're part of the way there. Ambition for its own sake is not a route to happiness, but if it helps you get where you want to be, you stand a good chance of fulfilling your potential and reaching contentment in the process.

Pundit

David Moyes spent a successful spell at Preston North End before taking the high-profile job of Everton manager in the Premiership. Recognized as one of the bright young talents in the world of management, he's conscious of the fact that ambition has to be tempered by making the right move at the right time. While still at Preston he was offered other jobs, but took his time to make the right decision; this is what he thought back then:

I'm extremely ambitious, I want if possible some day to manage at the highest level that I can and I want to try and have the right career path. I'm only 38 and I want to try and be in this game as long as some of the other managers and I have had one or two opportunities that I felt, at present, maybe weren't quite right for David Moyes, but in time when the right job and the right opportunity comes, then I would need to consider that.

Tactics

- Ambition is a powerful personal achievement tool, but it can be dangerous too.
- Over-ambition can lead to cheating – you may get caught!
- We can be more or less ambitious according to the culture we operate in.
- Sometimes, ambition can be influenced by social factors (like in the 1980s).
- Build your own 'pyramid' and decide what's at the top and bottom – it'll give you a clear idea of your goals.

▪ Be your own person and fight for the goals you believe in, not someone else's.

No one hands you Cups on a plate. (Terry McDermott – ex-Liverpool player)

3

Passion

Sound Bite

'Be still my beating heart.'

There's plenty of 'passion 'in football; it's everywhere you look – if only the same were true in business. It's on the pitch, where committed players push themselves to the limit to achieve their goal and be part of a winning team. It's in the stands, packed full of passionate supporters, cheering their team on through everything the British winter can throw at them. Who knows, it may also be in the fluttering hearts of the football groupies who pursue their favourite players in night clubs, because, let's face it, passion is sexy.

But in real life, as in football, 'passion' can fade and grow stale, it can be used for good or evil, it can be our friend or foe. In this chapter, we look at the importance of passion on the field of play and in the boardroom, because if we are to achieve our goals, it can be our greatest asset.

It's important to remember that PASSION and BELIEF are inextricably linked together; we can't be passionate about something we don't have wholehearted commitment to, and it's not something that can be handed down from manager to player. Equally, if we find we have belief in something, whether it be a football club or an organization, 'passion' will surely follow.

Pundit

Here's what ex-England Captain Bryan Robson thinks about passion: 'In any profession you've got to have passion and love for the thing that you're doing. I think the more desire you have the better chance you've got of reaching the top, whatever you're in.'

The importance of passion

- Strength and endurance – when everyone else wants to give up, passion is the thing that drives some individuals on to greater heights.
- Leadership – enthusing other people with your passion will help them see your vision and give them BELIEF in the goal you are trying to achieve together.
- Fulfilment – pursuing and eventually attaining what we believe in is a route to happiness like no other and passion can be the vehicle we use to drive us on.
- Inspiration – even when others don't share our passion for something, they can be inspired by our single-minded attitude and approach to achievement.
- Comfort – when other things around us are going wrong it can be a great consolation to fall back on something we feel passionately about.

Pundit

'Passion is important because football is tribal warfare, nothing less than that.' (Stuart Hall – BBC football commentator and lifelong football fan)

On the Ball

The danger of passion

An Englishman working in Zimbabwe was told to get his boss's car serviced and in order to do this he had to drive the luxurious saloon

50 miles to the next large town, where a suitable dealer could be found. As he travelled through the townships, many people came out of their humble shacks and stood by the roadside to watch the prestigious vehicle pass by.

During the journey, the man realized that the next time he passed through to get the car serviced in a year's time, many of the people would have died through lack of clean drinking water. Angered at the injustice of this, he resolved to do what he could to contribute towards the building of wells to prevent what he saw as needless loss of life.

He became consumed by a passion to fulfil this need and returned to England. Ultimately he drove himself so hard that he suffered a nervous breakdown, believing along the way that he could single-handedly solve the problem.

Where does passion spring from?

There are many sources of passion and often it is a number of factors combining that will produce the reaction we're more familiar with on the pitch than in the management meeting.

Heredity

Were your parents passionate people, did they champion any causes, what was it that energized them? Just as intelligence, looks, creativity and many other traits can be passed on from one generation to the next, so can passion. And it's just as likely that this will happen through a combination of genetics and environment; that's to say you may inherit the 'passion gene' from them, but equally important is the observation of their behaviours and the value system by which they rear you. You are more likely literally to *learn* to be passionate.

Circumstance

Fighting against the odds, having something to prove and over-coming adversity are all circumstances that bring out passion in people. The 'minnows' of the lower divisions who somehow play far above themselves in the early rounds of the FA Cup are a great example of this. The desire to show the world that they are every bit as good as anyone else keeps tired legs running and defences stoical. Similarly, organizations in crisis can pull themselves through if their people are passionate.

Peer pressure

The tribal behaviours that often accompany the moments of truth in a football match can stir the passions of all concerned. We've all witnessed the pre-match group huddle where players form a tight circle with arms around each other's shoulders in a gesture of defiance, 'together we will not be beaten'. Equally, the goal celebrations of hugging, back slapping and adulation stir the passions of the players and the crowd.

What does passion look like?

It's unlikely that passion will just pass you by without you noticing; it's just too powerful for that. But, if you stop to think what it looks like in other people, it's much more likely that you'll be able to convey your own passions more effectively to others.

Passionate behaviour involves the whole body. Someone with an all-consuming desire will signal through their movements a high level of commitment to their cause. Often these signs can look aggressive in nature, but as humans we are able to distinguish the subtle differences that make us aware that this 'mock aggression' is directed towards a goal rather than as a threat to us.

'Clenched fists', 'frowning', 'bared teeth', 'strained muscles', 'feet planted apart', 'arm waving', 'punching the air' and 'slamming down a fist' are the behaviours we often associate with passion.

One theory that goes some way to explaining all this is that passion at its height can mimic anger from a physiological point of view. The feelings we experience at moments of high passion stimulate our biochemical system, causing a release of adrenaline, and this reflects itself outwardly in many of the ways we've described above.

Passion usually explodes on the football field when a goal is scored; the player himself shouts and screams, does cartwheels, back-flips or spectacular dives, is subsequently 'mugged' by his own teammates and even these days kisses the badge on the front of his shirt to show loyalty to the club and solidarity with the fans (before being transferred the next week!).

Aware of the importance of the goal celebration, many players have taken it to extremes, performing almost tribal rituals that are either a private joke or a covert signal that becomes their trademark.

Paolo di Canio is widely recognized as the founder of the shirt front pulled up over the head and arms outstretched celebration, now so much in favour in school playgrounds and on Hackney Marshes on a Sunday morning. Not all celebrations have caught the imagination in the same way, and some one-offs have landed the perpetrators in trouble:

- Paul Merson mimicked the drinking of large quantities of beer before admitting to his alcohol-related problems.
- Robbie Fowler fell foul of the authorities when he knelt and 'snorted' the touchline, seemingly as if it were cocaine.
- Paul Gascoigne enraged Celtic fans when he pretended to celebrate by playing the flute, unknowingly causing offence through its origins in the Orange marches.

But this release of passion and its attendant behaviours is only part of the story; passion can equally well be expressed when talking.

'Passionate speech' has its own characteristics. It varies in pace from fast to slow and back again, often with key phrases repeated (think of how political leaders do this); and pitch can vary just as much as pace, with lots of rise and fall in the voice, something skilled exponents use to keep the attention and interest of their audience. But passion is not all shouting and screaming; sometimes impassioned speakers will play with our emotions and can make just as powerful a point by speaking very softly as by shouting.

In a footballing context there will be many occasions when you can see passion being played out, but one of the most intense is during the 'half-time team talk'.

Contrary to popular belief, this is not all screaming and shouting, though doubtless any professional footballer reading this would think of times when they could refute that! At the top level of football, a half-time dressing room is full of extremely rich and talented young men from all corners of the world. Their backgrounds and upbringing are all different, their cultures diverse, so to think that a bawling out during the interval is going to motivate all players equally is just too simplistic. However, great coaches will use 'passion' subtly to motivate their players before they return to the fray in the second half. Later in the text you'll find a section which contrasts the styles of two of the Premiership's most successful managers.

How do we get more passion?

With everything we've said so far about passion, you could be forgiven for thinking that it's something we've got or we haven't. Yes, that's true to an extent, but we can have a conscious influence over the level of commitment we feel.

You've heard people say, 'it's not something I could get passionate about' or 'this is an issue I can feel quite passionate over', so this suggests that there is a degree of 'whipping up' which can occur; it's something we do have some control over.

Training Tip

Fifteen minutes to greater passion

Use this exercise to discover your inner passion and how to fire it.

Take five minutes out to think of an issue that has disturbed you in the past; it can be big or small, from children starving on the other side of the world to teenagers dropping litter or dog walkers not clearing up after their animals. In the next five minutes write down the reasons you think this is the case: poor education, a lack of respect for others, a selfish society, etc.

In the final five minutes try to come up with list of solutions or remedies which could be implemented if enough people had the will and saw the world your way.

By now you should find that your heart is beating faster and your ire is raised. As well as physiological changes, you'll probably be thinking more clearly and feel a desire for change.

So, you can control your level of passion, just by taking the time out to think about how it can and should be directed. Try using this technique the next time you need to convince your colleagues of a viewpoint that's close to your heart.

A word of warning though, the high of passion can often be followed by exhaustion and an accompanying low. Maybe this is nature's way of giving us time to reflect on what's gone before, but whatever the reason, you soon come to realize that passion, for all its high energy and buzz, can wear you out. As Yoda from *Star Wars* says about 'the force', use it wisely!

Extra time and the extra mile

It's the final of a major championship and before you take to the field you're committed to giving every ounce of your effort for the full 90 minutes. This you do, covering every blade of grass on the pitch in the process, but when the final whistle blows the game is still a draw. At the point of exhaustion, what is it other than passion that will see you through? Compare and contrast this with a work-based scenario.

In business, with a target to hit or a deadline to meet in what seems like impossible conditions, what can you draw on to inspire you and your team, other than the belief that what you're doing is the right thing? Under these circumstances you are fuelled by passion.

One of the things that often characterizes this most powerful of emotions is *adversity*. Our desire to overcome this and right a wrong is often the source of our most inspired thinking and behaviour.

Football managers and coaches know this only too well, which is why one of the psychological ploys that is most often used is to cast their own team as the underdog; as well as increasing pressure on the so-called favourites, it inspires a 'we'll show them' attitude in their team. Similarly, in competitive environments, business managers can inspire their staff with the same technique.

On the Ball

Passion as the mother of invention

An inventor from Birmingham was driven by the desire to overcome a life-threatening adversity. As the so-called 'superbug' MRSA claimed more and more lives of hospital patients, many of whom had been admitted for minor procedures, he saw a flaw in the care system.

Although conclusive proof was hard to establish, it seemed that MRSA was transmitted from one patient to another in circumstances where wounds were open, and most experts agreed that fastidious cleanliness would go a long way to preventing cross-infection. Hand washing, latex gloves and throw-away aprons became a fixture of all wards, but still the death toll grew.

His invention of a fast-change disposable privacy curtain, which would stop the bed space being potentially surrounded by the bug, looked like being part of the answer, but the road ahead was fraught with problems.

Passion carried him through many levels of adversity, from devising and investing in a completely new manufacturing system through to breaking down the bureaucracy and outdated practices of the health service. He believed the product itself worked and would make a significant contribution to curbing the disease, he believed that as individuals we all deserve to have access to something which might prevent illness and he believed in the people around him who helped get the new system up and running. Without this burning passion the invention would have failed at the first hurdle.

Another example of passion at work in an unusual environment is given overleaf.

On the Ball

Climbing to the top

Bear Grylls is the youngest Briton to have climbed Mount Everest and survived, and he says this:

I wanted to give up every single day, but you get to a point where it's no longer about you; if you were on your own you'd have quit ages ago, but you end up doing it for the people you're with – you simply can't let them down. It works in reverse too, they're doing it for you, so you get through it together.

So, what do we know about passion? It's powerful but potentially exhausting, we can control it or be controlled by it, and it can be used for a variety of purposes, not all of which are good.

How then do we define, harness and purse our own passions in a way that will benefit us most? When passion so often leads to fulfilment, how do we get the best out of it?

Training Tip

Defining your personal passion

The first step is to indulge in a bit of self-analysis to determine just what your current passions are. This is no more complicated than taking some quiet time to yourself with a sheet of blank paper. Don't be restricted to writing down the passions in just one aspect of your life, for example work, or you'll end up channelling all your energy into a single stream of your existence.

Use headings like 'people', 'leisure', 'work', 'injustice', and think about whether your passions are local or global. After 10 or 15 minutes you will have a variety of subjects in front of you, some of which you actively pursue and get pleasure out of, and some which continually frustrate you because you never seem to find the time to do them.

There are only so many hours in the day, so all of us doubtless have passions that go unfulfilled. In this exercise, *choose three things that you are actively going to pursue in the coming months and put a time limit in place and a target for each.*

Try to balance the different areas of your life; you may choose to champion a particular cause, maybe a charity or helping out with a community group. In a work situation, it might be that you're continually frustrated by an outdated process and believe it can be streamlined, saving everyone time and effort; but balance this with something that's enjoyable too, like a hobby that you've always felt you have never pursued properly, such as photography, fishing or even football.

Your 'action plan for passion' is a way of raising the level of consciousness you have for the things you really feel strongly about. This will help you to take positive action and really become involved. The goals you set and the timescale you decide on are up to you, but try to be realistic in the first instance; if and when you achieve what you set out to do, there are plenty more passions you can indulge in.

One of the greatest side-effects of this type of thinking is that it gives you the opportunity to get your working and private lives in harmony; too much of one or the other can be bad for you, and by spreading your passionate behaviour across a range of subjects, you can take solace in the success you have in one area if things aren't going according to plan in another.

Love and loyalty

There is a romantic aspect to passion that can lead to love. This is true in our relationships but it can also spill over into other areas of life: 'He did it because of his love of the game', 'I love working for this company', but as we know, sadly not all relationships work out and over time we can grow apart.

There's a growing feeling that loyalty to our employer isn't what it used to be; we simply no longer have the passion, but is that a cause for concern or should we just accept it? Here are some of the factors that have brought about this change.

Back in my day...

Only a generation or two ago, there was a lot more loyalty between player and club, employee and employer, but lots of things have changed in society at large which have had an impact on that. It's not that we've all become much more shallow and self-centred, or that organizations don't care about us any more, but the way we live our lives has changed and that's had a dramatic effect on the relationship we have with whoever we work for. Here are some reasons why people believe we are neither as passionate nor loyal as we used to be:

- *Mobility* – on a local, national and global basis we are all more mobile and as such are prepared to go and seek work in different locations, no longer constrained by the hinterland of our birth.
- *Availability* – when you've got the world to choose from (if you're that adventurous) you no longer suffer from the usual troubles associated with supply and demand. If there is insufficient demand for your skills and services in the surrounding area, greater mobility (see above) allows you to overcome the problem.
- *Awareness* – technology and communications mean that we now know what's going on everywhere in the world, whenever we want. That increases our choice in just about everything, including work.
- *Competition* – a lot of philanthropy has been forced out of business, simply because it's become more competitive; this leaves little room for sentimentality and decisions about personnel are often taken solely on business grounds. That reduces any sense of 'loyalty' from the employer and the reaction of employees is to lower their expectations and faithfulness.
- *Aspiration* – the competition between companies is matched by the way individuals treat each other in some arenas. By trying to be better than the next person, we seek out opportunities to fast-track ourselves and get ahead.
- *Pressure* – external influences from everything, including the media at large, to a more localized expectation within our own peer group place more pressure on us to 'get on' rather than waiting for a first-team place or a promotion to supervisory level; we'll take our chances elsewhere.

In the real world

We all feel a glow inside when we hear the story of a young boy who has supported his local team from childhood and eventually gets the chance to play for them. Naturally under these conditions you might expect a greater degree of loyalty, but is it realistic to expect that at all costs? If the player gets an opportunity to join a better team, fulfil a personal ambition like taking part in a Cup Final, or (as is more often the case) earn a lot more money elsewhere, can we really blame him for sacrificing some loyalty? In the workplace too, employers only expect so much, especially when on their side of the bargain they no longer offer the 'job for life' which engendered so much loyalty in their employees a couple of generations ago.

Result?

All this could lead us to the conclusion that no one cares who their masters are, as long as there's plenty of money in it, but it appears both on the football field and in the workplace that this isn't the case. It would seem that both employers and employees are prepared to display a kind of transient loyalty to each other, a 'relationship of convenience' that suits both parties, for the time being, and a wider realization that this is unlikely to be for life.

One of the upsides of this is that the acrimony that has often accompanied a parting of the ways has subsided to a large extent. A Premiership manager who is losing the star striker he's coached from boyhood may rue the day he signs for a bigger club, but has probably known all along that this time would come. The best and most realistic organizations make contingency plans to make the parting as easy as possible. A West Country cider maker used to pay its sales staff two months' salary at the end of their first month of work; in that way, they were always paid up to the end of their notice period, meaning that when one of the team handed their notice in, they could ask them to leave the same day, which reduced the risk of taking the company 'secrets' to a competitor. Because everyone knew this was the case, there was rarely, if ever, any bad feeling on either side.

In business management, there can even be a sense of pride in having groomed an employee and given him or her the necessary skills to make his or her way in the open market of employment. In many senses, on both sides of the bargain we have swapped 'employment' (in the long term) for 'employability' (a skills-based asset, where we learn the things that will make us attractive in the job market).

Pundit

The last word on passion goes to Barry Fry, one of football management's most colourful characters, who's taken charge of clubs including Birmingham City and Peterborough. His own passion is evident, but the way he uses it to get the best out of players is an inspiration, even if the journey can sometimes be a rocky one:

I think it's a passionate game, I'm totally passionate and committed to the cause and I want my players to be; I think players have their own standards, they set their own standards; it's our job in a way to try to get their top standard consistently for a period of time and it's very, very hard to do that.

When they fall below that standard, I sometimes have a go; if they're having a bad game (it can happen to everybody), I try to get a reaction out of them and that's all I try to do, get a reaction out of them and if I call them an 'empty shirt' or something and they come back to me it doesn't worry me, that's my way, I just want them to change the attitude they had in the first 45 because it wasn't good enough.

So I don't mind people having a go at me about anything; we're all in it together sort of thing, I've thrown tea over people, they've thrown it back over me, it's the passion.

Tactics

▩ Passion is powerful; it's one of the greatest motivators.
▩ Heredity, circumstance and peer pressure can all contribute to our passions.
▩ An explosion of passion can help us achieve more than we thought.
▩ With time, effort and planning you can control your passions.
▩ People are inspired by passionate leaders – they have the ability to engender belief.
▩ It's fine to feel passionate and loyal at work, but don't lose your perspective.

These are players – men who play with their heads and their hearts. (Ferenc Puskas – former Real Madrid player)

4

Stress

'*Don't make me angry... you wouldn't like me when I'm angry!*'

In earlier chapters we've looked at some of the elements that are essential to the 'beautiful game' and which are of equal benefit in business. Having skill is essential, adding ambition is highly desirable and injecting passion (with some degree of control) goes much of the way to turning you into a winner. Get all these things in line and surely nothing can stop you; or can it?

Despite all the positive energy you're generating, you can (and sometimes will) fall prey to negative influences and the most commonplace of these is stress. How you cope with this, the behaviours you exhibit when under stress and what you learn from the experience can go a long way to completing you as a player, a business executive, a person.

How can *you* be stressed?

When top professional footballers and managers show signs of stress the media brands them 'whingers'. With all that money, how can they possibly be suffering from stress? But as all the scientific reports show, there is no correlation between wealth and happiness; in fact a recent study reported that even when earnings are doubled there was nothing but a short-term impact on how 'happy' people felt. Being able to buy more 'stuff' doesn't make you more fulfilled.

Broadcaster Eammon Holmes quotes the wisdom of his father when he said, 'there are no pockets in a shroud'.

What causes stress?

Stress is a very personal thing; not only can it vary from one individual to another, but changes in circumstances, mood and timing can significantly affect how we cope with it.

This is partly illustrated by experiments done on mice that show how our daily cycle or biorhythm can alter our coping skills according to when the stress is applied. Scientists placed a mouse in a large tin container, much like a biscuit tin, and attached a bell-like device to the outside; when they pressed the bell, the clapper rattled against the side of the tin, causing a deafening noise inside which came as something of a shock to the mouse.

They repeated the exercise at different times of the day, discovering that at certain points, when the mouse was at a low ebb, the noise of the bell literally shocked it to death. At other times when the mouse was more alert, the coping mechanism was sufficiently strong to withstand the shock.

As humans we are aware of the same kind of cycle in our daily lives. Situations that bother us a little during the day can become monumental if we wake in the night and start to worry about them; indeed, which of us hasn't been able to relate to the statement 'the darkest hour is just before dawn'. Our personal sense of perspective can swing wildly according to how fit our coping mechanisms are during any 24-hour cycle.

This daily pattern can form part of a larger picture, with a longer cycle of stress being brought about by a variety of different experiences. In order of significance, here are our top five causes of stress:

1. bereavement;
2. divorce;
3. redundancy;
4. moving house;
5. being beaten by Man Utd!

If we go through a period in our lives where two or more of the top stressors coincide, then our coping mechanism can be stretched to the limit, but under most circumstances we cope. It is very often only some time afterwards, when we look back on what we've experienced, that we can get some perspective, and in many cases people will say that with the benefit of hindsight, they don't know how they got through it. It is a testament to the human condition that we develop coping mechanisms that kick in during a crisis, but it is equally important to note that operating under stressful conditions for a sustained period is likely to result in damage in some form, if we find no way of reducing the pressure; in essence, there has to be light at the end of the tunnel.

Although our ability to cope with stress can be linked to the kind of personality we have, there are other factors which can increase or decrease the amount of pressure we feel we are under. In the workplace, this can be summed up by looking at Karasek's job control model. Professor Karasek has specialized in the study of psychosocial aspects of work, looking specifically at the issue of stress.

His model recognizes that there are three major factors which affect the amount of stress we feel. These are demand, control and support.

The 'demand' part is all about what is expected of us in our role, 'control' covers the amount of influence we have over the demand: is it in our power to alter how much we have to achieve within a certain time? And finally 'support', as the name suggests, refers to the amount of outside help we might expect from our network of peers and co-workers.

Below we've outlined two case studies using this model, the first in the world of football, the second in business.

Case study 1: Stress model and football

Imagine you are a professional footballer. You are single-minded because you are driven by a love of the game and you have a natural aptitude for it. For as long as you can remember, you have played and loved football, and now you have achieved part of your ambition by turning professional. Your goal in life is to make the very best of your talents, to enjoy the game and attract the recognition of your ability from peers, fans, the manager and your loved ones.

But, how much *control* do you have? Here are some of the factors you may be able to influence.

Lifestyle

There are many pressures on players who are young, fit, good looking and rich, not least of which is the attention of the tabloid press. Although it's a difficult choice to make, you can lead a lifestyle that doesn't involve nightclubs and alcohol, choosing instead to dedicate yourself to the game.

Fitness

Who's the first one to turn up to training and the last to leave? What do you do to build up strength and stamina, and how much effort do you put in to take you beyond your 'natural' level of fitness?

In a big competition, when the 90 minutes are up and the game unresolved, will you be the hero with the additional reserves of fitness to help your side win in extra time?

Skill

'Natural ability' will take you so far, but only the very arrogant or very foolish believe they've got nothing to learn. Study of the game, listening to a trusted mentor, and trying and applying new techniques are all within your control. Getting better is achievable if you practise to get better.

Dedication/effort

We make conscious decisions all the time about how much effort we are prepared to put into improving what we do. Many professional athletes are self-sacrificing to a very large degree, spending much of their lives dedicated to being the best in their field. Mental strength, determination and ambition sound like inborn character traits, but you can exercise some control by surrounding yourself with the kind of people who will encourage you in this.

What is *outside your control*?

Team selection

You can do everything within your power on the training ground, but all of that counts for nothing if you don't get picked to play on a Saturday afternoon. Some would say that you do have a degree of control over this, but no matter how much you 'let your football do the talking', there may still be times when it goes unnoticed. In today's game, it's sometimes inevitable that you won't play, as most clubs operate a rotation system, resting some players, even for key matches, so they have the chance to shine when they're picked.

Clubs are increasingly understanding the 'player life cycle', and as individuals reach what is euphemistically termed 'the autumn of their career', it may be that they simply cannot play every game any more and even when they do, reliance on tactics and 'thinking' a good game become more significant, as their ability to match the fitness of younger players wanes.

Other talent

Even if you have a regular first-team place, the future is still uncertain. Staying competitive means that your club will constantly be on the lookout for new talent, so even if you are the first name to go on the team sheet this week, it may be that a new player is about to join the club who will take your place.

Personalities and politics

Football, like business, is largely centred around relationships. When people issues are involved, it's inevitable sometimes that clashes of personality will ensue and decisions will be taken for dubious self-serving reasons from time to time. Getting caught in the 'political crossfire' can be one of the most uncomfortable feelings, especially if you have little or no influence over the outcome; it can be tremendously frustrating to be caught up in someone else's games when you were simply an innocent bystander.

Opposition

You can maintain a degree of control of your own circumstances, you can exercise influence on the people near you, both players and coaches, but the external factor you can do nothing about is 'the opposition'. Apart from anything else, it changes week to week and a strategy that may work in one set of circumstances is bound to fail in others. Just think about the playing styles of different Premiership teams and you can see how tactics (and often team selection) need to vary to cope with each different adversary.

Officials

'Football is a game played with 22 men and 40,000 referees'; yes, everybody thinks they know best, but you have only one person you are accountable to when it comes to staying within the rules of the game. You can't control who will referee your match or what their prejudices are (favourable or otherwise), nor can you account for whether or not they'll have a good game. It's not surprising then that all players will be a victim of a bad decision at some time or another and although we may accept this as part of the game, there's a certain frustration at not being able to control it.

How much *support* can you call on?

There are many potential areas of support for professional players; at the base level there are family members and friends who can be trusted for their advice. Premiership clubs have an intricate network of support 'services' available for players, from physiotherapists to fitness and nutrition experts, trainers, financial advisers, even someone to help them settle in, if they are relocating.

Using these services to the full means that individuals can remove many of the elements of stress in their lives and concentrate on what they're best at, playing football.

Case study 2: Stress model and business management

You're in a middle management position, responsible for a team of six staff of varying levels. Your own boss reports directly to the board of directors. You have been in your post for two years and have so far done well. There are a number of career options open to you, but you will need to make a move within the next 18 months or you may become 'typecast'.

How much *control* do you have?

Decision making

You have the power to make day-to-day decisions regarding the running of your department, although your degree of autonomy is limited by how you dovetail with other parts of the business, otherwise you will be accused of managing within your own operational 'silo' irrespective of the needs of others.

There is some leeway for getting it right by first getting it wrong, as many of the individual decisions you make aren't in themselves critical to business survival. However, the cumulative effect of your actions can either damage your reputation or turn you into a star.

People management

There's a framework of operation, but once more you have a degree of autonomy in the way you run your team. Motivating people and getting them to give a bit extra is about the personal relationships you are able to form and managing to balance those with each other and the needs of the business. You can use both 'stick' and 'carrot', but within the cultural context of the organization as a whole.

Budget allocation

How you handle your annual budget is up to you, but it's a fine balancing act between making sure you are sufficiently well resourced and not overspending. There is additional pressure from your team to spend the cash wisely, as much of your budget allocation is quite visible to them and they can see when you're making trade-offs between different budget lines. If you spend too much on 'hardware' and not enough on motivating them through incentives, then levels of enthusiasm will drop, causing a consequent downturn in performance.

Personal development

Apart from the additional learning you can take up outside office hours, you are free to apply for secondments within the company and have a high degree of influence on where your boss invests his or her training and development budget, which can have a direct effect on your learning. By volunteering to take on extra responsibility (like covering for colleagues/boss when they're on holiday) you have an opportunity to grow your personal skills base.

What is *outside your control?*

Policy making

Strategy is developed at the top level of the organization and this can have a dramatic effect on what you are trying to achieve day to day. Although you can make decisions without constantly referring them upwards, this is only within the boundaries of company policy. If your views about the running of the business clash with the current strategy, then the upshot will be extra stress.

Top management structure

The threat of merger or takeover and the possibility of management moves above you are outside your control. The most dramatic effect would be if your own boss were to be replaced, but changes at board level could alter the strategic direction of the organization and this has its own set of challenges (see above).

Competitor activity

No matter how hard you work or how well you motivate your team, if the competitors have found a way of doing what you do better, cheaper or faster, then you'll have to run just to stand still. Finding ways of monitoring what they're doing will mitigate some of the risk, but only if your own management are prepared to listen to what you have to say and take action to combat what is happening in the marketplace.

External forces

Inflation, economic depression and the war on terrorism are part of the mix of political, environmental and social factors that you can do little about, yet they will affect the success of the business as a whole and logically your part in it. When trading is poor, it's hard not to be brought down, and when that happens it's even more difficult to motivate those around you; the result is stress.

How much *support* can you call on?

As with the example of the footballer earlier, we tend first and foremost to turn to those close to us for support; this might be a spouse, a trusted friend or another family member. The way this plays out in reality can vary widely, from getting practical help to do our job, to a 'listening ear' for us to unburden the pressures of the day.

Organizations too offer support; however, the level of this is variable. It may be that a robust structure is in place with sufficient staff at the right level for you to be able to delegate (incidentally, if you don't do this, you only have yourself to blame), or you might have the flexibility to buy in additional effort on a temporary basis to help out during busy periods. Your peer group may also be very supportive, covering for you at meetings or sharing some of your workload.

The best organizations understand the need for pastoral care too and benefit from being caring by keeping their staff healthier and more productive. Occupational health departments are becoming more commonplace and some employers even offer their staff confidential counselling services, through outsourced workplace counselling services and employee assistance programmes (EAPs).

Finally, once again company culture plays a big part in the level of support we feel we're getting. In very macho cultures, people are more afraid to admit to stress, as it may be interpreted that they can't cope. Alternatively, some organizations offer 'stress management training' courses, so that all staff get the chance to understand the signs of overwork and are more likely to be able to spot it in a colleague or even themselves.

More than just control

From these two case studies, you can see parallel factors in football and business that can contribute to a rise in stress levels. This is partly brought about by demand, either from the organization/football club, market factors, or by the pressures we exert on ourselves to succeed.

It's increasingly common for us to put greater pressure on ourselves than our employer demands, but this is just one symptom of a society that is 'results driven'. Apart from peer recognition, we usually feel as though success will bring financial reward (which is certainly true in football), and as a society we erroneously equate money with happiness.

What might the effect of these extra pressures be? In *football* terms it may mean playing while injured, by having a pain-killing injection before the game; in *business* we might fall prey to a long-hours culture, so by arriving earlier and staying later we (in theory) get more done. But in both of these cases, logic would suggest that our ambition is writing cheques that our physiology can't continue to cash. Instead we simply put today's demands (physical, emotional, spiritual) on a kind of quality-of-life credit card, in the hope that we'll be able to pay it off in future.

We've seen that the final part of the job control model is *support*, which covers the human infrastructure we build around us as social animals. In stress situations, support can come from the sources we expect, like family, friends and peers, but sometimes it can be outside that group, from a stranger, if they spot the signs of stress in us.

Paradoxically, it is sometimes the case that the 'support' network turns against us, causing an increase in the stress we feel. An example might be business managers who have too many demands on their time. They fall victim to the long-hours culture and soon the work/life balance falls badly out of kilter. Without a sympathetic partner, the situation will be made a lot worse, so finishing work late, then returning home to face a barrage of abuse will cause stress levels to rise even higher.

On the other hand, peer group support can mitigate this and it is often the people who are in the same position, or who feel 'there but for the grace of God…', who are most sympathetic.

This kind of camaraderie can be seen at its height on the football pitch, where team members will rally round if one player is having a tough time and support their colleague until the worst of the crisis is over. Think about the striker who has suffered a goal drought; the more games he goes without scoring, the more he will need the support of his team-mates, but when he does finally find the back of the net, it's likely that his peers will join him in the joyful celebration, sharing in the delight as they did in the despair.

Stress relief

The reason we've gone into some detail on the Karasek model is that it gives us a framework for starting to work on relieving stress. It's only when we can understand where the stress is coming from that we can start to deal with it in an effective way.

The simple answer is to find ways of reducing demand and/or increasing control and support.

Demand

Part of the problem most people have in reducing demand is that they think that even the desire to do so is a sign of weakness. Rather than admitting to themselves and others that they can't cope, they'll carry on regardless until they reach breaking point. This macho attitude is now very outdated, as we now recognize stress as a real and significant problem in all walks of life. Often it's cumulative demand that takes the toll, so no single task is outside the ability of the individual; it's just that when you add them together, the strain becomes too much.

In football, the team captain who's suffering a personal dip in form at a time when his club are in the relegation zone and facing financial worries may start to feel the burden of responsibility. If other demands are placed on him, like a commitment to help with the organization's PR by working in the community, an agreement with the team's sponsors to attend a number of events and the continual demands of the media to delve into the minutiae of his personal life, it may get to the point where it is simply too much.

Similarly in business, the manager who is understaffed, with higher than ever targets to hit in shorter and shorter timescales with less and less resources, is going to suffer a similar fate.

In both cases, the entire infrastructure of the person can come tumbling down like a house of cards; if the demands are not reduced, it's often the case that a small event or request can cause 'breakdown' to occur, just like the straw that breaks the proverbial camel's back. You may have experienced this in others; a seemingly small error causes them to explode into a fit of fury, disproportionate to the amount of aggravation it might have caused.

Control

We've seen how lack of control is a major part of the stress model, but just how little control do you have? In the preceding paragraphs we've talked about work/life balance and how you can shift that, but many people feel as though they can't take the big decisions because of the potential negative impact that might have.

To exercise some influence over the demand equation we have not only to be prepared to put our hand up and stay 'stop', but we need also to be able to recognize when we are being expected to do too much.

Most people work better with some pressure, so it can be a fine balance to judge when demand is getting too high; however, if you've reached the stage where there is no gap in between your 'busy periods' to rest and recuperate, then danger could lie ahead; copeable pressure turns into damaging stress!

Training Tip

Controlling the demand

The first step to self-diagnosis is to audit the demands that are placed on you. This is no more complicated than taking 10 or 15 minutes out to have a think about the way you're living your life. It might help if you jot down the different 'sources' of demand and the expectations of each, which should result in your having a comprehensive list of what others expect of you. Just knowing where you stand can be a revelation, and it is often after this stage of the process that people start to make conscious decisions about how they want to change the future.

Once you can start to see the wood from the trees, the next step is to prioritize the demands that face you. Only you can decide what the most important thing is, but don't be put off by what other people think, as the result will be that you fail to manage demand effectively. If you are passionate about work success then go for it, but negotiate this strategy at home to make sure the demand level falls there. Alternatively, if spending more time with your family is first priority, you need to explain to them (and your employer) that this is your intention and be aware of the fact that this might mean a radical rethink of your lifestyle, even a change of career. Stories now abound of stockbrokers turned plumbers who have 'sacrificed' their career in the City for a simpler, less stressful (albeit less lucrative) life.

The classic scenario is well-paid business managers who work long hours but have all the material trappings of success. They may not want to break the news to their children that by downshifting their career they may have to put up with having fewer 'goodies', but set that against being able to spend more time together and even if the financial sums don't stack up quite so well, the emotional ones will.

Another strategy that will help is if you find ways of delegating the demands that are upon you. This might be on a one-off basis, like asking a colleague to host this week's sales meeting so that you have time to prepare for appraisals; or it may be ongoing, like agreeing with your children that they need to take responsibility for getting themselves up and ready for school without your input.

Planning is a further ploy which can help to manage demand. You'll know this to be the case if you've ever suffered from 'headless chicken' or 'blue-arsed fly' syndrome. Having a prioritized list of things to do with a time span allocated to each is a great way of reducing the stress of demand.

When you've done all this you'll be in a position to see some of your problems more clearly, and often at this stage you will come to realize the amount of time taken up with pointless activities that add no value to anyone, either you, your peers, family, friends or the business you work for. Stop doing these things and no one will notice; well, that's not strictly true, you'll be the one to notice when you have a bit more time on your hands.

On the Ball

Bin the bull

Lady Marie Stubbs is famous for having come out of retirement to take on the demands of a difficult school which had been placed in what's called 'special measures' by Ofsted. Part of her philosophy included putting all the paperwork she thought didn't directly affect the learning and welfare of the pupils to one side. She said, 'if I left it there and no one had come back and asked about it 12 months later, it went straight in the bin!'

In work scenarios it's often the culture of the organization that prevents individuals from feeling in control. If everyone around you is behaving in a certain way it can be tough to be the one to stand up and say you're going to do it differently. But this doesn't have to be done in a way that threatens discipline, if you can come up with a sound rationale for speaking out and suggest different ways of doing things in future. Taking a collective stance against a practice that causes stress to many people can result in a positive outcome, especially when a more collaborative approach can result in work being more fairly divided.

The final thing to remember is that you shouldn't underestimate the power of a one-to-one discussion with your immediate superior. Managers aren't mind-readers and often if you are prepared to discuss the stresses you are feeling and talk in an open and honest way about the lack of control you feel, you may find that they are sympathetic to your situation and will negotiate a more balanced approach for the future.

Support

When it comes to support, you reap what you sow. The more prepared you are to help others out at a time when they need your support, the more likely they are to reciprocate. This doesn't mean you take on their tasks for them, in fact that's only likely to end up with you suffering from stress instead, but often all people need to know to be able to deal with their own stress is that someone else recognizes the problem.

Let's go back to the striker in the midst of his goal drought. No one else can break his personal deadlock and score for him, but because so much of the problem is to do with confidence, a mental attitude, rather than physical fitness or skill, knowing that his team mates are behind him can make a huge difference. Under such circumstances, he is much more liable to take the opportunities presented to him, rather than shying away from shooting chances, and consequently break the deadlock.

As a manager you'll get respect from your team if you take the time to look at the world through *their* eyes now and again and acknowledge the challenges they face.

Pundit

If you're very lucky in life you might get to a situation where you can leave the normal stresses of work behind. Gordon Strachan had a successful career as both player and manager, but recognizes the toll of high-level stress over a sustained period and before leaving Premiership club Southampton had this to say about his future:

This will be my last job as a manager. I hope to do it as long as I can and then retire from I would say the high-profile jobs, the high-pressure jobs; still stay in football but coach at a level where you can enjoy every day, because there's no way you can enjoy every day as a football manager; the only time you really enjoy yourself is when you've won a game of football, so I'd like to get in a position where I could enjoy every day, without any real stress.

Obviously there's stress in most jobs you do, but I'm talking about the high-profile stress.

Tactics

- Stress can come from many sources and can be affected by heredity and our daily cycle.
- High demands and a lack of control can significantly increase stress.
- Support from others helps to reduce our stress levels.
- Work/life balance is a critical issue for today's business professionals.
- We can control the demands upon us by better planning and prioritization.
- Supporting others is likely to encourage them to do the same for us.

It was a game of two halves and we were rubbish in both of them. (Brian Horton – former Oxford United manager)

5

Discipline

'Dreams are what get you started. Discipline is what keeps you going.'

When we think of discipline related to ourselves, the tendency is to equate it with self-control, but when applied to others the term can have rather negative connotations; it sounds more like the application of 'stick to the rear end' than the enticement of a 'carrot at the front'. But whatever our interpretation, discipline is just as important an element in both football and business environments. We start this chapter by looking at our own ability to be disciplined.

The elements of self-discipline

Fit for purpose

We've already touched on one aspect of fitness and we know that too much alcohol, too many cigarettes and takeaways is no way to stay in shape and that applies equally well in business as in football. Looking after yourself physically is just as important if you're going into battle at work as on the field of play. Keeping fit physically has an effect not just on how we feel, physically, but also in terms of our self-esteem.

There's a second important element to fitness. In our subheading above we've included the words 'for purpose' because 'fitness in business' goes beyond just the physical state we're in. We also need to consider how well prepared we are for our role. This might involve you taking some time out to think about how you could be better at your job, what kind of additional training you might need and how well informed you are.

Control

In the last chapter on stress, we looked in detail at the issue of control in terms of how others can alter the course of our working day; here we're more interested in the sort of control we need to exercise over ourselves if we are going to perform at maximum efficiency.

Self-control means taking objective decisions in a rational manner, with the emphasis on outcomes, not personalities. Balancing the needs of the individual, the team and the business takes fine judgement, and if we exercise control in these areas, it's more likely we'll get the outcome we're looking for.

But self-control can be difficult, because it often means doing what's right as against what we instinctively want. In business this could be as innocuous as wanting to join the conversation round the coffee machine about last night's telly highlights, when the time 'wasted' could be better utilized emptying the e-mail inbox.

The word 'wasted' is highlighted because there are occasions when this kind of social activity may be beneficial; it might mean we have an opportunity to relate to other members of the team, or it could be a natural gap between the tasks we have to perform that day and so act as a de-stressing agent.

But control means exercising your judgement about these things.

Anger management

There are things in working life that wind all of us up, but discipline is about finding ways of dealing with them. Sometimes we get frustrated by systems, the inefficiency of the tools we use, or the lack of a valuable resource we need to do our jobs. All of the energy spent getting angry about these things is debilitating, so you need to ask just one question, 'do I have the power to change this?'

If the answer is 'yes', then start right away, because the longer you leave it, the more opportunities there will be for you to become frustrated and you will be distracted from whatever you're doing. If IT is the problem (and when isn't it?), invest in getting the right hardware and software to do the job. Too often people waste time and effort in finding 'ways around the system' when it is the system itself that is at fault; get it fixed, then you can stop worrying. It may be that the only thing that is at fault is user inefficiency, so you have to be prepared to put your hand up and ask for further training. Very often the time and money spent on getting up to speed on a frequently used system is repaid many times by the time it saves (and the reduction in your blood pressure!).

If the answer to the question is 'no', and you don't have the power to change things, then recognize this state of affairs and do everything you can to move on. Worrying about the situation any further is pointless.

Self-motivation

Other people will make varying attempts to motivate you at work, but the truth about management is that you're mostly left to do the motivating yourself. What is it that gets you out of bed on cold winter mornings and heading off to work? If one day is much like the next and it seems you are not achieving much, it's going to be hard to stay motivated. Often this is to do with having no clear idea of what you're trying to achieve on any given day, so you go through the motions, simply marking time until the next day comes along.

Get rid of this fuzziness by setting daily objectives that contribute towards the greater goal. These can include 'positive steps' or 'blockage removal'. An example might be a sales target that needs to be hit; positive steps could include calling all current clients to see if you can persuade them to increase the size of their orders, or compiling a database of lapsed customers to whom you can write.

'Blockage removal' is more to do with clearing the decks so you can spend more time taking positive steps; this might include dealing with mundane admin tasks or persuading internal departments to increase productivity.

By applying self-discipline to these tasks you'll get a lot more done, but the critical final step is to take five minutes at the end of each day to review your achievements so that you'll feel both satisfied with what you've done and inspired to start the process over again tomorrow.

The reason all this is so important is that as either a footballer or a business manager, you are in a position of some responsibility and other people will look up to you. This might be for guidance or as a role model, but either way you need to be accountable for your actions and set an example to others, whether they're fellow players and fans or colleagues and stakeholders.

The message you're sending out is 'this is the way we conduct ourselves around here, it's professional and businesslike and the expectation is that everyone associated with the club/company will behave to similar high standards of self-discipline'.

Now there's an opportunity to find out how self-disciplined you are by taking this quiz. Are you ice-man or volatile, Mr Spock or lost-the-plot?

1. How would you typify your temper?
   a. lose it easily, but quickly calm down again;
   b. never lose it, but sulk instead;
   c. rarely lose it but boy does everyone know it when you do!;
   d. pretty much of an even keel all the time.
2. If other people could use a few short words to describe your temperament, which would they pick:
   a. cool and calm;
   b. highly strung;
   c. loud and extrovert;
   d. reserved and quiet?
3. You're playing in the FA Cup Final and just before the end of the first half, one of your teammates is sent off for a foul he didn't commit. Do you:
   a. remonstrate with the referee and insist he consults the fourth official;
   b. channel your energy into calming down other members of your team;
   c. kick the opposing player who feigned the foul;
   d. breathe deeply and try to get yourself back under control?
4. The server has crashed again at work and you can't get into your e-mail for the third time this week. Do you:
   a. bang your monitor as hard as you can with your fist;
   b. resolve to get on with other things until it's fixed;
   c. ring the head of IT and verbally abuse him or her;
   d. call a meeting of interested parties to see if a solution can be found?
5. One of your teammates is late for training and the reason is obvious, he's been out on the tiles the night before. How do you react?
   a. ignore it, we all like to enjoy ourselves sometimes;
   b. ask loudly, 'what time do you call this?'
   c. lead the rest of the team in a chorus of 'why are we waiting?'
   d. resolve to get on with training and have a quiet word with him afterwards.
6. Your supplier's JIT ('just in time') delivery turns up JTFL (just too f*****g late!); do you:
   a. get a colleague to hold the driver while you punch him;
   b. cancel the contract and find another supplier;
   c. shrug and put it down to experience;
   d. ask for reasons why they're late again?

7. How often do you indulge yourself in your vices:
   a. sometimes;
   b. often;
   c. rarely;
   d. occasionally?
8. Your attitude to going to the gym is:
   a. a pain but it has to be done;
   b. a way of working out your anger;
   c. part of being a professional;
   d. avoid it at all costs.

How did you score?

Question 1. a = 2, b = 1, c = 3, d = 4
Question 2. a = 4, b = 2, c = 3, d = 1
Question 3. a = 2, b = 4, c = 1, d = 3
Question 4. a = 2, b = 3, c = 1, d = 4
Question 5. a = 3, b = 2, c = 1, d = 4
Question 6. a = 1, b = 3, c = 2, d = 4
Question 7. a = 2, b = 1, c = 4, d = 3
Question 8. a = 3, b = 2, c = 4, d = 1

What does it mean?

If you scored between 25 and 32

There's no need to panic, but then again, because you're so in control it's very unlikely that you ever do. You have mastered the art of coping in adversity, and are able to handle the most stressful situations without 'losing it'.

When all around have lost their heads, you are the voice of reason, you stay focused on the task and when necessary hold a post-mortem after the crisis has subsided, to make sure the same thing never happens again.

Take care though, you could become too detached. The result is that you'll appear to show little or no emotion, no matter what happens, and this could be potentially damaging in two ways. First, you may lose empathy with other team members; yes, they may respect your ability to keep your cool, but soon they might start to wonder if you care at all. Secondly, you risk suppressing your innate passion, and we've seen before what a powerful tool this can be in your make-up.

Try to balance your desire to stay in control without losing touch with your natural feelings; you don't have to rant and rave, but at least show that you give a damn now and again.

If you scored between 17 and 24

Most of the time you are on top of your game and people around you are surprised if you lose your cool.

Although it's occasionally obvious when things have got to you, you don't take it out on the innocent victims nearby. You care enough to express your opinions and are at ease with your own assertiveness, but you are mostly able to keep a lid on your anger.

Resist the urge to 'button up' altogether or you will be suppressing a healthy and emotionally sensitive side of your personality, which is something you're going to need if you want to really engage with your teammates and colleagues.

If you scored between 8 and 16

Talk about 'light the blue touch paper...!' Your fuse simply couldn't be any shorter, so maybe it's time for an anger management course... that's supposing you don't want to pick a fight with the tutor!

Chill out; not only are you causing yourself undue stress, but you're setting a bad example to others, especially the people who look up to you.

When things go wrong, use the old trick of counting to 10, then try to apply some logic to the problem. By the time you've solved the immediate crisis, you'll have probably calmed down some and may be in a position to delve deeper into what caused it in the first place (which *still* doesn't give you the right to hit someone!).

Discipline and performance management

There are rules in every game and breaking them usually results in punishment.

In football there is a sliding scale according to the severity of the incident. Breaking a rule like being caught offside results in no personal black mark against the perpetrator, but some benefit is given to the other party in the form of a free kick, thus penalizing the team as a whole.

More serious offences, like fouls, carry stiffer and more personal penalties with the guilty party being shown a yellow or sometimes red card, depending on the severity and/or frequency of the offence. In the season 2002/3, there were 1,900 red card offences and a massive 30,000 yellows.

On the Ball

A shooting chance

Occasionally, when discipline gets slack, a referee may need to revert to more severe measures to restore order. This story, originally from the South African Press Association, later appeared in *Private Eye*:

'The dispute began when the referee awarded a penalty against the visiting team', policewoman Mali Govender told a press conference in Kenton-on-Sea, in South Africa's Eastern Cape. *'Some of the Marcelle players protested and objected when the referee gave one of them a yellow card. An argument broke out, and some of the Marcelle fans stormed the field. That was when the referee pulled out a firearm and began shooting. He shot the Marcelle coach dead, and wounded two of their players, then ran off the pitch screaming "I am now the master of the universe" and has not been seen since. We are hunting for him, but he is still on the run. We don't know what his tactics are, because we haven't found him yet.'*

Later, the South Africa Football Association issued a statement: *'It was with regret that Safa learnt of the fatal shooting of a coach and the injuries to players in a soccer match. However, the referee that officiated in this match was not a properly qualified official registered with Safa, he was one of the spectators who had been asked by the organizers to handle the match. Furthermore, we should like to put on record that the match between Ekuphumuleni and Marcelle was an unofficial village friendly that was not played under the structures of Safa and we are therefore in no way responsible. Safa passes its condolences to the family of the coach and wishes a speedy recovery to the injured players.'*

A rather extreme example of tough discipline we'll admit, but what are rules and regulations for in the first place? Most importantly, they provide a structure for the game, one which is easily understood and universal, so each team has to abide by the same guidelines. Next, the rules are designed to ensure fair play, to give both sides a solid framework that outlaws cheating. Finally, the rules act as protection against harm; they're designed to stop dangerous play and protect footballers from injury (clearly they are not always successful in this).

Rules are in place for the benefit of everybody and for the smooth running of the game.

Pundit

During a long and successful career in club management, Graham Taylor has formed his opinions on how to keep discipline within a team; sometimes it has to be balanced with individual creativity, but without being heavy handed he believes that players need to know what the 'structure' they're working within is:

I don't know any successful team that isn't organized, whether it's by the manager or by the players themselves on the pitch. I think that a manager has to lead, he has to be prepared to make decisions knowing that he's not going to get every one right; people look not necessarily for discipline, but a structure where they know that is what is expected of them; it's not that they're not allowed to go out of that structure but there are consequences if they do.

Although the same applies in business, it's all a bit more vague. Certainly it's true that the laws of the land set some kind of framework around lots of important areas like health and safety, fair trading and discrimination; compliance with these issues is a more and more onerous task for businesses, but the individual rules that companies set for themselves have much more leeway.

Often it is organizational culture that points the way to the rules, 'that's just the way we do things around here', and most companies would benefit from a more explicit set of guidelines, like we see in football. Certainly any industrial tribunal judge would support that course of action, as most of the arguments put forward by companies in such cases revolve around the implicit expectation of behaviour, rather than some explicit instruction that has been given.

In many cases, individual judgements of what is and isn't allowable and the penalty that should be paid for contravening these rules are down to the discretion of the business manager, so just how do you decide what is fair?

Guidelines for discipline

Circumstances vary widely, organizations have different things to achieve, and culture, as we've seen, has a strong influence on what's thought to be right and wrong; with so many variable factors it's impossible for us to develop a set of rules that you should use as part of your management style. Instead, we've given below some pointers towards the kind of issues you need to consider when setting a disciplinary framework for your staff.

Before you launch headlong into drawing up a rulebook, think about the implications of getting it wrong. Too much discipline and you'll lose the faith of your team; they may react at first by doing what you say, but their motivation will be damaged, possibly resulting in some of them quitting altogether. When new people come in they'll be 'poisoned' against you by the remaining members of the team. Nothing will happen without a negotiation first and goodwill (eg asking someone to stay late and finish an important job) will evaporate.

Conversely, too little discipline has its own set of problems. Motivation is likely to be an issue again, but for a different reason. Under these circumstances some team members will observe that 'you can get away with murder here' and doubtless will spot the weakest link in the team who is doing just that; for example, if one member of staff is consistently late and the issue is not addressed, this has an effect not only on their own role (which suffers because they have less of a working day to do it in), but also on their colleagues, who will no doubt have to cover for the work that's not being done.

Requests for extra effort at busy times will be met with derision and there will be no way of enforcing change; people will just revert to their old ways. What is even worse is that once this pattern has been established, it's very hard to reverse, simply because past precedent will make a proposed tougher regime seem unreasonable.

At worst, organizations with slack discipline and poor systems have fallen prey to criminal activity on a scale that ranges from a fiddled expense claim to wholesale fraud involving millions of pounds.

Here are some factors to consider when outlining the rules.

Rationale

What reasons have you got for drawing up this new set of guidelines? If you can't think of good ones, then it'll be impossible to 'sell' the idea to other members of staff. If you stop and think about Health and Safety rules as an example, it's easy to see that there's a sound rationale behind them; they're in place to stop people from getting hurt.

So, if you were to introduce a rule that says the four members of your team have to stagger their lunch break, a good reason would be that important customer enquiries are continually put through to your department and to achieve a better level of service and satisfaction, you've decided that the phones should be manned throughout the working day.

Appropriateness

The work environment isn't a boot camp (unless of course you work in a boot camp!), so suddenly trying to impose a 'zero tolerance' policy is likely to look heavy handed. At the same time, you need to be careful not just to follow precedent as this will mean nothing changes. When you come up with a new rule, think about the degree of change it will mean for people and then check your rationale (see above) to measure if it is appropriate to what you're trying to achieve as a department and in the wider context of the company as a whole.

Clarity

'No one told me' must be the most overused defence when it all goes horribly wrong. Even minor changes need to be outlined in a clear and concise way and some written confirmation is always a good idea. You don't need to be heavy handed about this: you can call a team meeting, talk through the new practices and then follow up with an e-mail covering the important points.

This is the stage where you'll find your preparation useful, as you'll be able to present a sound rationale for the changes and defend their level of appropriateness in line with business need.

Parity

Apart from the fact that the law forbids it, you can't impose dual standards on your team. Whatever new rules are to apply, they need to be universal and it's often useful if you include yourself in the changes. So, if we return to our example of the lunchtime cover for incoming calls, you're more likely to get support if you don't have an 'opt out' clause for yourself that allows you to swan off for long lunches with your management peers!

Consistency

You've done the hard part of preparing for change and then 'selling' the idea to your people, but the implementation phase is vital. First, you have to stick to your word (so if you've agreed a policy on punctuality at meetings, don't let someone off the hook at the first sign of lateness) and then you have to keep on sticking to it.

People will equate a lack of consistency with a lack of parity and will see your actions as favouritism; even worse, they'll think it's simply not fair, and fairness is an absolutely critical cast-iron element of a successful disciplinary policy.

Reasonableness

Outside the armed forces, it's rare that discipline is black and white. In fact, even in football, there are many shades of grey, which gives managers something to complain about on *Match of the Day* and the tabloids something to write about on a Monday morning.

Applying hard and fast rules and never allowing any leeway isn't likely to make you the most popular boss in the world, but find a good reason for 'letting someone off'. If you have a new mum returning to work after having her first baby, cut her a bit of slack for a while; the rest of the team will understand, be sympathetic and see you as more compassionate. In the end, we all make our own judgements of what is reasonable; see what you think of the following example.

Think about this

There are eight people in the sales team, all of whom have company cars so they can visit customers at their own premises. Once a month each person has to complete a mileage form (as part of Inland Revenue regulations) stating their business mileage. The company has a rule that if the forms aren't submitted by the 15th day of the month, they will assume a 'standard mileage' and charge the individual £200 for private mileage, to be deducted from their next salary.

Missing the deadline has a knock-on effect on admin staff, personnel (for their record keeping) and finance, who have to process the claims.

Carol has a reputation for always being a day or two late, and when a new manager takes over he is made aware of the situation. After calling a team meeting to re-emphasize the policy, the reasons behind it and the implications of late submission, Carol misses the deadline once again; she pleads for some leeway, based on the fact that the previous manager usually allowed a day or two's grace. She also promises that it won't happen again, but despite this her new boss fines her anyway.

Reasonable or not? You decide.

This is a real-life scenario and the opinions of the eight members of the team ranged from outrage (at Carol's end of the spectrum) through to 'serves her right' at Jan's end. Incidentally, Jan used to work in admin and had to process late submissions!

Pundit

I think in football, as a manager, organizational skills have got to be spot on, the same as in business, and I think motivation's got to be right too, but most of all you've got to have discipline within the club or company. You do that by involving people in the discipline code that you're going to instil, whether it's staff or the players, and the rules have got to be for everybody, not just for individuals.

Of course if people have problems then it's different because you've got to handle each individual case when it comes along, but overall, as far as discipline's concerned, the code should be the same for everybody. (Bryan Robson, ex-England captain)

Crime and punishment

So, we've talked a lot about setting the boundaries for discipline, but what happens when someone (like Carol) oversteps the mark; how exactly do you deal with that?

During a match, just about the only thing you can do is shout from the touchline, but your entreaties are likely to go unheard or unheeded, so better to save your breath and consider how to deal with the problem later.

There's an important lesson here for business managers too; bawling out a member of staff in the full glare of the rest of the team when tempers are at their height is probably the least professional behaviour you can possibly display.

Calm down

Disciplinary action of any kind should take place when the heat has gone out of a situation. You may be dealing with an angry and upset employee, or you may be feeling these emotions yourself. At best, you won't be as rational as you can be, and at worst may, to coin a cliché, 'say something you'll regret'.

Training Tip

A measured response

If necessary, sleep on the problem and see if you still feel as annoyed the next day; if you do, try to analyse why: did the perpetrator let you down, undermine you, cause grief for colleagues? What is it about their behaviour that's raised your hackles? Sorting this out in your own head will help you to see both the problem and the solution.

Let's say they openly criticized a decision you'd made in front of the team, ending with 'I always said that wouldn't work'. Here are some reasons you might be angry:

■ You're the boss and you expect respect.
■ You're afraid they might be right, it was a bad decision.
■ It's all gone wrong because of their negative attitude.
■ They've chosen an inappropriate time and place to criticize you.
■ Theirs is not to reason why.
■ The decision may have been unpopular but it was necessary.
■ They are only saying that because you were promoted ahead of them.
■ How dare they criticize you.
■ Their decisions are just as bad, it's a case of the pot calling the kettle black.
■ You've been in this business for much longer than them, what do they know?
■ The decision has caused some teething problems but you can resolve these.
■ If the team pulls together a solution can be found.
■ Your authority has been undermined.
■ They are plain wrong, the decision was a good one.
■ You've never liked them much anyway.
■ They resent your success.

Go back through the list and decide in each case whether the reason is driven by emotion or fact/opinion.

It may be that some of the negative feelings you're experiencing are based on emotion, maybe you simply don't get along with this person, but the lesson to learn is that you have to put this to one side when you come to the disciplinary procedure. You need to base your discussion in *fact*, rather than *emotion*.

This isn't to say that you're not allowed to recognize openly the feelings you're experiencing, but the foundation has to be what has actually happened. You could therefore say, 'I know my decision has caused some teething problems, but I think we can work out a solution between us; however, when you criticize me so openly, without us having the chance to discuss it first, I get frustrated about the effect that might have on the morale of the team.'

Face to face

If you've got something to say, then go ahead and say it. Not many of us openly relish the prospect of conflict; it raises our stress level and can leave us feeling upset. Yet, there are times when not addressing an issue causes us more angst; by simply storing it up inside us it continues to bother us in the longer term.

However, avoiding the issue by sending some form of written communication doesn't work. Apart from anything else, it doesn't give the other person the right of reply (at least not immediately).

Old-fashioned (and unenlightened) managers used to do this all the time in 'memo' format, which has largely disappeared from today's businesses, but the memo did at least have the advantage of not being instant. It used to be said that if you'd written a memo in anger, you should put it in your top drawer, read it again the following day and only send it if you still felt the same. Sadly the rise of e-mail has put paid to that; with the advent of the 'do-it-now-and-press-send' culture, people are being bollocked right, left and centre and not always justifiably.

Better then to find a quiet place where you won't be overheard, ensure you're not going to be interrupted, sit down face to face with the bollockee and get on with it.

Don't shilly-shally about, come straight to the point with the reason for the meeting and then manage his or her expectation of what is coming next. Say that you intend to outline the reasons why you thought his or her action was out of order and he or she will then have the opportunity to have their say, after which you'll come to a decision about whether further disciplinary action needs to follow.

Pundit

A final word on this subject comes from Mickey Adams, whose management career has included spells at Nottingham Forest and Fulham, as well as 110 games in charge of Leicester City. Here, he describes his personal management style:

Hard, but fair, I think the better managers are. I don't think there are any grey areas with me, I think players understand where I come from and what I want from them and providing I'm fair with everybody and everybody adheres to the same rule then I'm more than happy to go along with that.

Tactics

- Discipline starts with you; try to stay in control of the situation.
- Plan the tasks for each day and review your progress before leaving work.
- Rules are there for everyone's benefit, but think carefully before you instigate changes to them.
- Fairness is extremely important; you must treat all staff with parity.
- In a disciplinary situation deal with the facts, not the emotions.
- Handle delicate matters face to face if you want to clear the air.

People say a good referee is one the fans don't notice but that's a myth. If a referee has to give three penalties in a match, then he is going to be noticed. That doesn't mean he's not a good referee. (Pierluigi Collina – Italian referee)

The Second Half

6

Captaincy

Sound Bite

'Clowns to the left of me, jokers to the right, here I am stuck in the middle.'

We head into the 'second half', having spent the 'first 45' looking at your individual skills, attributes and aspirations. This next section is more about the roles you are likely to encounter, like coaching and management, as well as taking a look at how to select your best team and what to do about the opposition. We start, though, with one of the most crucial roles of the game, *captaincy*.

It may be that you aspire to become chief executive of the company you work for, to set up your own enterprise, with you as the head, or to one day inherit Daddy's business and run it your way. Whatever your goal, it'll help you no end if you've spent a spell of your career as team captain. We've chosen to analyse this role because the captain has a curious kind of middle-management position within a football club, and many of the traits that typify great football captains can be found in great captains of industry.

The chapter's broken down into sections that look at what the role of captain entails, the qualifications, skills and experience you need to become one and how you apply this to the real world of football, or business. Hopefully this will help if you're early in your career and aspire to management; if you're already at the mid-stage and managing people, you should see instant parallels between your role and the football captain, and if you're running the business, this should emphasize the need for you to select and retain a good 'captain'. In fact, whether you're reporting to it, doing it or managing it, the captain is a vital role.

What do captains do?

Good captains are middlemen, acting as both a conduit and a buffer. They take up the halfway position between the rest of the team and the club management, which is not always a comfortable place to be. Sometimes, in conduit mode, they are translating and interpreting the messages from one side to the other, maybe instructing players in their strategic role within the team, or feeding back the mood on the pitch to the dugout. When the going gets tough, they act as a 'buffer', absorbing the fears and angst of either side and passing on their concerns to the other party in a measured way.

Middle managers in business do this all the time, taking the 'orders' of their superiors and translating them into a form of words more palatable to their work colleagues, or alternatively distilling the gripes and moans of their fellow workers into a coherent concern for management to address. To do this they have to speak two languages (at least!), that of the boardroom and of the 'shop floor'; using the wrong one in the wrong place can have disastrous consequences. It's like being abroad and thinking you've ordered the prawn cocktail, only to find that the snails turn up.

On the Ball

Learning the lingo

Lynn Rutter is an international businesswoman having worked at the most senior level within Nokia and Oxfam, but on the way up she found you have to adapt your language to survive:

I didn't go to university and my first job was working for Green Shield Stamps as a tea trolley lady. That helped to form my communications skills in a great way, because I was working alongside glorious people like Flo and Gladys; they were the salt of the earth trolley ladies and the last thing you want to do is to come across as some stuck-up middle-class kid.

So, you learn very fast to listen to people and pick up on what they're saying and communicate at the various levels that they need you to communicate at. I don't mean to say that these people were not bright, but they didn't have an academic vocabulary, so there was no point in talking on a highfaluting level. You had to talk in a straightforward and under-standable way – and I guess that was a very good lesson.

So, it's not a matter of talking 'up' or talking 'down' to a particular group, it's about using the right language and being mindful of how easy it can be to patronize people. As a lesson, this following quotation was heard across a busy open-plan office: 'Come here a minute and let me just sit you down and explain in a simple fashion what patronizing means.'

If you find yourself in circumstances where you're confused about what language to use, then opt for PLAIN. This doesn't have to be blunt or rude; it just involves saying what you mean. Often people who use flowery, academic or intellectual language are just trying to mask the fact that they don't know what they're talking about.

Have you got what it takes?

What are the traits of great captains and managers? Here are the things that we think are important.

Authority

Team captains have authority in a quite unusual way. A good way of describing them would be to call them 'first among equals'. In fact, if you're sitting in the stand watching the team on the pitch, it's pretty hard to tell who's captain at first glance – everyone seems to be playing an equal part. It's only when you get close up and see the badge of authority of the captain's armband that his position becomes clear. This is an important point because often middle managers, like captains, form part of the team they're in charge of, which changes the dynamic of their authority and has serious implications for their management style.

Autonomy

You might think that this is the same as authority, but it differs in quite a subtle way. Before kick-off and after the final whistle has blown, the manager or coach has the ultimate authority over the team, but for the 90 minutes in between, the man *on* the pitch is the one who is best placed with the ability and strategic positioning to make minute-by-minute deci-sions that can turn the game. During this time, the captain has to interpret the instructions he's had from the manager and execute the game plan in the best way he knows how, but because he can't keep running back and forth to the bench he must make his own decisions on the hoof (or boot).

Sometimes this happens in business too, like for example at the front line of customer service. During busy periods in a retail environment, a team leader will have to make decisions that attempt to maximize customer satisfaction (the overall management game plan), without continually referring to 'them upstairs'. Once the shop is shut, the balance of power transfers back again and the leader (as with the captain) may be called upon to justify the decisions he or she made 'in the heat of battle'.

Many service-led organizations have wrestled with this issue in recent years, under the fancy name of 'empowerment'. This has challenged the 'totalitarian state' system that companies used to be run on, where no one had authority to stray outside the strict guidelines set down. This led in the old days to the birth of that much loved British institution the Jobsworth; 'I'm sorry mate, I can't let you in here, it's more than me job's worth.'

On the Ball

The great British Jobsworth

This football-related incident first appeared in *The Observer* in January 2004:

At Liverpool football club, they have a system called PTS – Priority Ticket Scheme – which, for about £50 a year, enables fans to phone up and buy tickets that are on general sale.

One duly attempted to ring on a Monday to obtain tickets for an Everton derby match but gave up frustrated after more than four hours and decided instead to go to the Anfield ticket office the next day. This is how the conversation at the window went.

FAN: Got any tickets for Everton left?
OFFICIAL: Yes, quite a few.
FAN: Can I have one? I'm on the PTS.
OFFICIAL: No, they are only on sale by phone.
FAN: But I tried doing that for four hours yesterday.
OFFICIAL: You couldn't have. But anyway, I can only sell you one if you phone up.
(At this point, the fan takes out his mobile phone and rings the office number. The phone beside the official rings.)
OFFICIAL: Good morning, Liverpool Football Club here, how may I help you?
FAN: It's me at the window. Can I have an Everton ticket please?

OFFICIAL: Yes sir, what's your PTS number?
FAN: Here. (He holds up his PTS card to the window for the official to see)
OFFICIAL: And how will you be paying, sir?
FAN: Credit card.
OFFICIAL: And the number?
(The fan holds up his credit card to the window)
OFFICIAL: Thank you sir, your ticket will be in the post.
FAN: Can't you just give it me here to save on the postage?
OFFICIAL: No sir, I'm not allowed to do that.

As service standards have got better, there's been a growing realization that you have to let front-line people make decisions about what is best for the sake of customer satisfaction, even if this has some kind of cash cost associated with it. Some organizations have gone as far as allocating a sum of money (say £100) to each member of front-line staff which they can spend in any way they like to 'delight' a customer. Giving people this discretionary spending power can eventually lead to them exercising discretionary behaviour, ie taking the initiative to 'do what's right' regardless of what the corporate rule book says.

You find the starkest examples of both good and bad in this regard in telephone-based services like banking and utilities.

Perspective

Imagine how different a game of football looks if you're the player manager on the pitch, as against the team coach sitting on the sidelines. Now think what the view from the stand would be in comparison and you can start to get an idea of how important perspective is.

Being on the pitch gives you a different view of things, but what is even more important is that you get the opportunity to pick up the moods, emotions and feelings that are part and parcel of the game. If there's a lot of anger in your team (maybe because of a bad refereeing decision), you have to harness that and turn it into passion; if the mood is downhearted (because you're losing), you need to inspire and lift the team. A few quiet, well-chosen words at the right time can work wonders, and the same applies in business.

Some experts think that perspective is so important it even matters which position the captain plays in.

Pundit

'Nine times out of ten, central defenders make the best captains as they can see everything in front of them and organize from the pitch.' (Emlyn Hughes – ex-England captain)

Dual role

One of the hardest parts of captaincy is that you're trying to hold down two jobs. As just another player on the team, you're doing what you can to contribute as positively as possible to the overall effort, but at the same time you need to be conscious of everything else that's going on around you and be thinking all the time about the subtle adjustments that need to be made in positional play, or saying the right word at the right time to get a fellow teammate to raise their game.

So, if that's what a captain does, how do you become one, what are the qualifications for the job?

Competency

As a manager you don't necessarily need to have the skill of an accomplished central defender or the pace of an old-fashioned winger; your talents are more cerebral and connected with strategy and tactics rather than your own personal fitness.

The same can't be said of the team captain. The base qualification is that you have to be recognized as being an expert in your own role; without this there is no way you will be able to act as an example to the rest of the team.

Similarly, in business management you do not need to be an expert in *all* the disciplines you're managing, but you do need to have a specialist skill that you are recognized for, something that other members of the team can look up to; from that springboard you can start to lead by example.

Experience

There are lots of things we can learn in life simply by applying ourselves to the task, but experience isn't one of them. You have to have been there, even if you didn't buy the T-shirt to prove it.

The one thing we can do to gain experience more quickly is to make a conscious effort to learn from both the positives and the negatives of what we do. In football terms this means taking time out, even after a thrashing, to look at what you could have done differently (as an individual and a team). As it's generally recognized that we can learn from our mistakes, most managers are happy to let us make them… once!

The great thing about experience is that it gives us a reference guide to what to do in times of adversity; we can think back and often recall similar circumstances, then instinctively know what the right course of action is. Over time, there is an even more useful benefit; even when faced with a totally new situation we can find *parallels* with the past that give us a basis for decision making. If you're the kind of person who looks for silver linings in every cloud, then take heart that even when things are bad, you're learning all the time.

Maturity

This is a trait that's linked to experience, but there is not always a direct correlation between the two. We've all heard the expression 'an old head on young shoulders' about a player who displays an uncharacteristic level of maturity for their tender years. In the same way, there are countless seasoned professionals around who still act as if they're in the playground at junior school; you're probably thinking of one now.

Being mature is about keeping a cool head in volatile situations, rising above the taunts of the opposition (players and fans), and having the ability to transfer that 'inner calm' to people close around you.

Impetuous displays of temper, tears and tantrums, pouting, sulking and whining are all out; *maturity is about overcoming your inner emotions and presenting a measured exterior to the world*. In the captain's position, it's likely that younger, less experienced players will look up to you, and for this reason, as much as any other, you have to set the right example.

Balance this with the fact that in business, as in football, you're allowed to show passion (in fact it's virtually compulsory), but this is a positive, focused, channelled behaviour, not a petulant tantrum.

Application of captaincy skills

If these are some of the qualifications that you'll need to become a great captain or business manager, how will you use them? What behaviours will you display on a day-to-day basis; what does the well-rounded team leader look like?

In a sentence, you'll be a self-effacing and empathetic professional with an ability to communicate on all levels; that's the sound bite, but what does it actually mean?

If you think of the great team captains of the past at club or country level, they all seem to manage to achieve the right balance between confidence and cockiness. To do the job at all, you have to believe in your own abilities and that self-confidence should be there for all to see, but it doesn't have to come about by you telling everyone how wonderful you are at every given opportunity. Very often the kind of people who do this lose credibility, because everyone else realizes that they're simply trying to mask their own low self-esteem.

In post-match interviews, model captains always give credit to the team as a whole and play down their own achievements. Which of the two following statements do you think you're most likely to hear? 'Yes, I was pleased to get the goal, but overall the team deserved the victory because of the hard work we put in across all areas of the pitch', or 'Yes, I was pleased to get the goal, you'll not see a better one than that scored in a long time… certainly not by someone as good looking as me.' You get the point.

The next adjective from the sound bite is 'empathy', being able to see the world from other team members' perspectives. You may have never played in goal, but if you're mature and experienced, you'll have the ability to put yourself in the keeper's shoes (or boots) and understand the problems he has to deal with. Even better, you'll be able to make *him* see that.

This is a key skill in business too; it's the gift of not only being able to understand the issues that other team members face, but also having the skill to show them that you do. There's nothing people hate more than someone saying 'I know just how you feel', when quite clearly they don't. One of the key elements of coaching is being able to hold back from suggesting a solution based on your experience and helping people find their own way of solving the difficulties they face; not only is this more rewarding for them, but it's far more likely that the learning will become embedded quickly and the mistakes will be left in the past.

Defining 'professionalism' in any meaningful way is difficult, but it's to do with how people conduct themselves, not only in public, but away from the glare of the spotlight too.

If you employed a solicitor who was the model of respectability in the courtroom, following the protocols of the legal system and maintaining the highest standards of discretion and client confidentiality, you'd still think them anything but professional if you later found out they'd been gossiping about you to all their friends in the pub. So the set of standards or values by which we live our lives and conduct ourselves in our chosen job are the criteria that other people will use to judge us.

Professionals in any sphere aren't putting it on, they're living it.

Finally, we turn to 'communication' in our analysis of great captaincy behaviours; this isn't just about knowing what to say and when to say it, though clearly that's very important, it's also, quite critically, about knowing *how* to say it.

Earlier we talked about the captain's piggy-in-the-middle role, which requires him to be both conduit and buffer. With both of these things the captain acts as a kind of translator, taking both the messages and the language used to deliver them and turning them into a form of words that the recipient will find more palatable. Without the empathy we mentioned before, in the example by Lynn Rutter, this would be impossible.

In many advertisements for face-to-face sales jobs, you'll find the expression 'must have the ability to communicate on all levels', and this is exactly what team captains and business managers need. If you cease to see people as individuals and communicate on the basis of always appealing to the 'lowest common denominator', it won't be long before you've lost the ear of everybody concerned.

We're talking about outbound communication here, but before you even get to the stage of opening your mouth, it's a great advantage to find out what other people think; in other words, shut up and listen!

Being a great listener takes time, effort and all your attention; we all hear what's going on around us, just by virtue of having ears placed on either side of our head, but the expert listener will pick up not only what's said on the lines, but what's going on between them. Often this is not about the words spoken, but the tone of voice, pace of the speaker and non-verbal expressions, like sighing or lack of eye contact.

Expectations of a team captain

Over time you can not only acquire the skills and experience to be a great captain, but also discover (as in our last section) how to apply what you've learned in the real world. Talking of which, here are some of the things that might be expected of you.

Ambassador

In amateur leagues, the team captain takes the role of a kind of special representative of the club, meeting and greeting the opposition and the officials. On the professional stage, this is more ritual than reality as there are staff on hand to make sure the away team and referee can find their dressing rooms and so on.

However, the ritual of the sporting handshake still takes place between the captains at the start of the game and they undertake this duty on behalf of their team mates; it symbolizes the intention of fair play (though after some games you might be left wondering why they bothered!).

In the same way, you might be expected to take the lead in a business situation, especially when any meeting and greeting needs to be done.

Exemplar

We've touched already on the role of the captain in setting an example and match officials will expect this to be the case. If a game is getting especially heated, the referee will often call the captains together, as representatives of their team, and tell them to calm things down.

Team captains who 'lose it' often cease to command respect from officials, managers, supporters and sometimes even their fellow players.

Spokesman

In a well-ordered team, the captain is expected to speak up on behalf of the other players; there is a recognition that at critical times in a match he must act as the voice of the players, especially when it comes to making representations to the referee. Similarly, back in the dressing room, while everybody is entitled to their say, the captain's opinion is seen as being representative of the view of the team. Sometimes, through indiscipline, this system fails completely and everyone shouts at once, but it soon becomes apparent that nothing is achieved in this way; we need leaders in every sphere and the captain's role is critical.

Although not everyone can be a captain all the time, having the experience of this, or a parallel business role, makes us much better at understanding the difficulties of handling people; ultimately, we become more sympathetic towards these problems and increasingly aware of the need to reach a compromise.

Pundit

I think what you need in any industry is to be honest with the people around you so you have a good relationship, but when you're the captain, if you think people are out of order you tell them right away.

Some people find it very difficult to tell others to their face exactly what they feel; well, I think if you're a captain you've got to, because if somebody is doing something disruptive the captain can sort that out at his level – it doesn't always have to go back to the manager.

When I was at Man United I got on well with all the lads and I never found a problem; it was the same when I was captain for England, and it goes back to that thing about honesty.' (Bryan Robson – ex-England captain)

Tactics

- The captain's role is critical in football, just as the team leader or middle manager is in business.
- There is a necessity to be able to speak the languages of 'both sides'.
- During 'moments of truth' (while the match is being played, or the 'shop' is open) the captain must take responsibility for what happens.
- Great captains tend to be competent, experienced and mature in their outlook.
- Emotional intelligence is an important asset to any captain; they need to be able to see the world from someone else's point of view.
- As a captain you need to strike a balance between confidence and cockiness.

The referee was bobbins. If you need that translating it means crap. (Dave Jones – former Southampton manager)

7

Coaching

'Don't tell me what I should do, tell me how I should think.'

Coaching would be easy if that was all you had to do, but in this chapter we recognize that in football, as in business, it's often only part of the job.

Specialist coaches are now fairly commonplace, but they have the advantage that they can just parachute in now and again, fulfil their obligation and ride off into the sunset again (what an exciting life they lead!).

The difficulty for the rest of us with coaching duties is that we have to cope with a 'day job' as well. What is even harder is that our 'other' job is sometimes even in conflict with the coaching role. If an individual in your team asked for coaching in the area of handling conflict, you might find over time that you were the cause of the conflict in the first place. It's difficult in that environment to get involved in a trusting and open session that involves positive feedback on both sides!

Pundit

Colin Todd made the move from 'Assistant' to Manager at Bradford City and thinks that coaching players, or 'man management', is a fine balancing act:

The big difference is the responsibility that they put on your shoulders; as a coach you're mainly the buffer for the manager, you take some of the responsibilities; now I take all the responsibilities and I have to accept that, so that's basically the main difference. The bigger aspect of it is man management, how we handle the players and how we get the best out of the players; you have a squad and it's how you handle the ones who aren't playing, the ones who are left out, because somewhere along the line you're going to need them again.

We've recognized that this is a dilemma, but it's something we have to learn to live with, so let's move on and look in more detail at the issue of coaching, safe in the knowledge that the complexities of the dual role may mean it's not always plain sailing.

In football, there is no single model of coaching, but clearly at a wealthier Premiership club there is room for specialist coaches, in goal keeping, forward and defensive play, etc, whereas clubs in lower divisions may not have this luxury.

So, you can see how the role of managers and coaches might vary according to the size of the club; what is commonplace is that whoever is coaching will have some influence, if not the ultimate say, over team selection. A conflict of interests is bound to arise from time to time.

Here's an example

You're coaching an out-and-out winger, but are worried that at the age of 32 he might be losing the pace that would have formerly taken him past any defender. In the later years of his career, you believe his interests are best served by pulling him inside to a central midfield position, but this will mean a radical rethink of his game. Having always played on the wing, and without the benefit of your objectivity, he can see no good reason for the change of role.

Because part of your job involves team selection and tactics, you can insist he plays where you tell him, but on the training ground on Monday morning it's hard to establish the kind of rapport you need to coach him effectively in his new position.

In business too, it's often part of the role of managers to engage in an ongoing coaching process with staff; in fact, it could be said that this is the most important part of any manager's job, facilitating other people's skills and bringing out their natural talents for the benefit of the team and the business as a whole.

What makes a good coach?

Think for a minute about the current clutch of coaches in the Premiership and ask yourself what they all have in common. Some are ex-players, others are not. Some are British, others are from abroad. Some come from working-class backgrounds, others are middle class. Some are young men, others are much older. So, coaching mustn't be governed by any of these factors; there must be other things at play which make them able to do the job well.

Pundit

David Moyes raised his profile as a coach when he took on the job at Everton; he thinks that 'getting qualified' is important, but having the hunger to keep on learning all the time is also vital and that's a lesson that applies in business, just as much as in football:

A lot's made of coaching qualifications now. I believe they're right – you can't expect just to fall out of football and think you can walk in; I think you do need some basic ideas. I've completed my new pro-licence in Scotland and I think that sometimes when you go into management maybe you think that's your job done and I've always tried to look for more information, find out new things in training or coaching, or I'd study diet, or psychology, whatever it may be; I think you must keep looking.

We've listed below some of the essential attributes of a good coach.

Knowledge

Coaching involves having a deep understanding of many things, including the 'psychology of the players', the 'skills' and 'abilities' of your own team and the opposition, and 'how to deal with conflict'.

But before you can put any of this into practice, you need to have a detailed and in-depth knowledge of the technical side of the game. Clearly the interpretation of this on the field of play is open to many variations, or else all teams would play the same; however, the basics of the game remain fixed.

You may be fooled into thinking that you'd have needed to play the game at the highest level yourself in order to understand this, but there are many examples of effective coaches who were never particularly gifted players. In fact, it can sometimes be a limiting factor if having spent a lifetime playing in one position, you're now called upon to coach players who occupy other bits of the pitch.

This can be an important point to remember in business, where there are still some people who don't recognize the emergence and importance of 'professional managers', ie people who can apply the techniques they've learnt to a variety of situations. It's no longer true that you have to have worked your way up from the 'shop floor' in order to be able to manage those people; what you do need to show is knowledge in your field, an ability to apply what you've learnt to a new and unfamiliar situation and empathy for the issues that the people you are coaching face.

Engagement

A huge part of being an effective coach is the ability to build 'trust' and 'rapport'. So, coaches have to be able to engage quickly with a whole variety of people, whose backgrounds, motivation, aspirations and sometimes language may not be in line with their own. A certain chameleon-like quality is needed in order to be able to adapt style and technique to each individual.

This is especially important because, as we'll see later, coaching is a process which requires people to be open and honest with themselves and the coach, and many are understandably nervous about being exposed in that way. It's highly unlikely they'll engage in the process if a high degree of trust hasn't been established right at the start.

Empathy

This is really a subdivision of engagement, as 'empathy' is about understanding what it is like to be the other person. That's easy in social situations with friends whom we have probably selected on the basis that we have lots in common with them. It's much harder when faced with a person who's come from a different social class, with a different set of values and a different outlook on life.

Imagination has a large part to play here, because although our experiences haven't been the same as the people we might be coaching, we really need to be able to 'walk a mile in their shoes' to get a grasp of what will motivate them.

As a man in his thirties you may hold down a position that requires you to manage a team of women-returners, who have taken a career break to have children. Without imagining the difficulties of balancing child care with home life and the pressure of a job, at a time when your physical and emotional resources may be stretched by the lack of sleep and other demands of a newborn, you may end up handling a whole range of issues with a lack of sensitivity.

So, in football an established and mature manager might have to deal with a clutch of very young, very rich (compared to their peers outside the game), very energetic young men. As we've mentioned before, the British tabloid press are at pains to point out how easy it is for situations to get out of control.

Modesty

Some football coaches have enjoyed iconic status during their playing careers and may well have been the schoolboy heroes of the players that end up in their charge. But coaching isn't about telling the other person how you did it when you were in his or her position. Coaches need to be self-effacing and switch the emphasis away from themselves and onto the individual who's the subject of their attention, rather than dwell on their own past glories.

So, we've now summarized some of the attributes of good coaches; but what exactly do they do with them, how do they turn this set of skills to practical use, what are the techniques we need to learn to be able to coach others?

A practical approach to coaching

Planning

Like many of our good intentions, coaching only happens if we plan to make it so. In a busy work environment, it's easy to let this kind of thing slip off the agenda. Football is much better at recognizing the importance of continual professional development, perhaps because the results are instantaneous and there for all to see, every Saturday afternoon. If your business had a similar hard and fast measure for success that it published every week, perhaps it would focus everyone's attention a little more.

The first thing that has to happen then, if coaching is to work, is that a plan must be drawn up by both parties, outlining the schedule. This needs to include time set aside on a regular basis, with an opportunity to review progress at set milestones.

Make sure that the really important junctions, like the main coaching and review sessions, are set in stone, otherwise they'll get 'bumped' by other priorities, but at the same time build in some flexibility to the system to allow for changes in circumstances.

Objectives

It should really be part of the plan to set objectives across a range of timescales. Rather than replicate business objectives (like, for example, a sales target), the idea is to introduce personal goals that will increase confidence and ultimately have an effect on the role and the work performance of the individual.

Pundit

Long seen as one of the 'nice guys' of the game, Harry Redknapp has still managed to prove that you can be effective at the same time, as any supporter of West Ham will testify:

A lot of the game is confidence; they'd all worked hard and even if results didn't go right it was never through lack of effort. It wasn't a case of suddenly knocking people and telling them what they couldn't do, it was always a case of making them believe that they were good enough to win the league and keeping the confidence high.

The whole point of coaching for the people who volunteer for it is that they already know where they want to be, but they can't see how to get there or to overcome the obstacles that are already apparent. For this reason, the emphasis should be on the person being coached to set the agenda and develop the objectives.

Clarity

Lots of organizations are so vague about what they're doing it's a wonder they continue to trade at all. What's worse is that by the time objectives are set at an individual level they're even fuzzier. The result is a lot of wasted time and effort as workers attempt to come to terms with their role; it's a situation that causes a lot of conflict too, because people are drawn into arguments over their interpretation of the plan versus their colleagues'. This is never more so than when 'territory' and 'power' are on the agenda. It's at this point that managers will battle fiercely with one another.

All of this needs to be borne in mind when you enter a new coaching 'contract' with someone. *A lot of negative behaviours can be avoided by making sure that the objectives are completely clear at the start and then checking back periodically to make sure you share the same understanding of what's been agreed.*

Because coaching is often regarded as a 'softer' skill, you may mistakenly think that objectives would be quite easy, but the balance that needs to be struck is to have goals that are challenging without being threatening.

Elements of a coaching session

Assuming that you have put all the important elements in place and the process of coaching has commenced, it's helpful to look at some of the things that will happen during the session.

Questioning

Coaching is not a process whereby you change someone else's thinking or behaviours, you are there simply to help them in the process of doing it for themselves. Your role is to aid their thinking, help them explore different avenues, encourage their curiosity and capture all of this so you can ensure some action planning takes place.

One of the key methods of achieving this is through questioning; try to make sure that questions are both open and emotive. What this means is not asking questions that could have a 'yes or no' answer, and making sure that you explore feelings, emotions, thoughts and aspirations, rather than simply ascertaining the facts of a situation.

Some examples of coaching questions are listed below to illustrate the point:

■ Tell me a bit about how that made you feel.
■ How did that affect your relationship?
■ Describe your emotions when you found out.
■ What do you want to happen?
■ How could you feel happier about the situation?

These are the sort of questions that will help you work out part of the problem; as people express their emotions you can discover what makes them upset, stressed or unhappy with the situation they are in.

From here you need to start to explore ways of finding solutions and, as we've said before, this doesn't mean you should start the next sentence with 'I'll tell you what you need to do…'

Instead, your questions need to focus on resolution:

■ What would make you feel differently?
■ How could a solution be found?
■ What other angles could you explore?
■ Outline the possibilities as you see them.

A very good practical way of getting answers to some of these questions is to use a *timeline technique*. You can physically mark a line on the floor (masking tape is good for this) and stand the individual at one end; this represents where we are now with the problems that we want to overcome. Next, walk them down to the other end of the line to where they want to be and ask them to describe their vision of the future. This might be 'I want to feel secure in my product knowledge, so that I don't make a fool of myself in front of clients'; in football it might be 'I want to be in a position where I don't get "shrugged off" the ball so easily.'

From here, it's much easier to look back down the line and think about the steps that need to be in place for the end objective to be achieved; the additional benefit is that you can see that progress must be made in stages, a bit like the milestones we referred to earlier.

Listening

Asking questions is the important first part of the process, but the next part is of equal or possibly even greater significance – you need to *listen* to the answers. To be able to do this will mean you'll need to keep quiet! – be on 'receive' rather than 'transmit'. We've already been at pains to establish that coaching is not a process where you give people advice based on your own vast experience, so you really need to be able to listen actively to what they are saying.

We're labouring the point, because there is a great temptation, if we've overcome our own difficulties in the past, to share that experience with others and even to tell them all the right and wrong things we did to achieve resolution.

Even when asked 'what would you do?', you need to step back and try to involve the other party in the solution, taking a collaborative approach to finding the answers.

Remember, as well, that there's a difference between passive and active listening; if you really concentrate you'll pick up not only what's being said but also what the underlying mood is. With experience, you'll get to judge when the way something is being said doesn't correlate with the words being spoken. For example, 'yes, that sounds like a great idea' spoken in a dull monotone would suggest the very opposite, but pace, tone, 'brightness' and rise and fall in speech patterns will all give clues to mood. Watch the person you're coaching closely and you'll pick up these signals.

Body language

Another giveaway in how people are feeling is their body language. If someone is telling you that they agree entirely with what you say, but at the same time they're sitting in a bunched-up pose, with arms folded and legs wrapped around each other, the chances are they really think you're talking rubbish.

In a coaching session, you need to take this on rather than ignore it, but you'll be much less confrontational if you're simply honest. Most of us are uncomfortable with conflict, so we tend to avoid it at all costs. However, a less threatening way of addressing the issue is to simply make two statements that seem to contradict each other and ask the other party if they can explain the apparent mismatch: 'I hear what you're saying, but I'm picking up some negative signals too; can you explain how you're feeling inside?'

Body language is important for another reason, because there are two people in the room; your own body language will convey all sorts of messages to the person you're coaching, so you need to be genuine in your approach or subconsciously you'll give yourself away.

Stay conscious of the way you're sitting, don't fidget, look at your watch or show any other signs of inattention. When you're in 'active listening' mode, try to remember to lean forward towards the other person, keep good eye contact, smile and nod agreement when appropriate. All of this will make your questioning easier, as you are displaying signs of genuine interest in the answers you're being given; the other person is more likely to be relaxed, and consequently give you an honest response.

Feedback

An important part of the coaching process, which is likely to come up during some sessions, is *feedback*. Far from being a euphemism for criticism, feedback should include positive experiences as well as negative. Used properly it is a valuable tool for developing constructive dialogue that results in the other party gaining insight into the way their actions and behaviours are affecting others.

Your role is to lead them on this 'voyage of discovery', reinforcing positive behaviours and highlighting areas to work on.

Feedback can spill over into criticism if it's handled badly, so here are a few things to avoid:

■ Don't give feedback when you're angry – wait until the heat has gone out of the situation.
■ Don't make personal comments; feedback is about actions and behaviours, not the way people look!
■ Don't make generalizations – keep feedback specific to avoid ambiguity.
■ Don't get dragged into apportioning blame – feedback should be about finding a positive way forward.
■ Don't make feedback irrelevant – avoid focusing on things that you have no influence over.

Rather than get drawn into some of these things, make feedback a positive experience by setting aside time for it and make sure you're not going to be interrupted. You should have prepared the other party by letting them know in advance what your intentions are, rather than just springing a feedback session on them. Here's a list of some other useful tips for handling feedback:

■ Do everything you can to keep things informal and relaxed; *feedback should be a dialogue, not a monologue.*
■ 'Bracket' any negatives with a positive either side, so start and finish by drawing out something good that's been achieved.
■ Describe what you've witnessed in the other person's behaviours and how those made you (and possibly others) feel.
■ Stay focused on specifics and give 'real-time' examples to illustrate your points wherever you can. Don't say 'you're always doing this or that…'
■ Manage the other person's expectation; you might not want to be interrupted while you go through the feedback, in which case you could say something like this: 'I've got three issues I want to give you feedback on, so I'll start by running through them all, then we'll come back and discuss each in turn.'
■ Offer plenty of opportunities to clarify understanding: 'Do you understand what I'm saying?', 'Can you see what I mean?'

When you've delivered the feedback, allow additional time for questions and discussion, invite a response and try to get the other party to suggest their own solutions, changes to behaviour and ways forward; that way they're much more likely to embrace them.

The final thing to say about feedback is that it is a two-way process in more ways than one. All feedback sessions should result in a discussion taking place, but as well as giving feedback to others we should welcome it ourselves. It may be that our presence or behaviour during a particular scenario has given cause for the other person to react in a negative way and we need to be able to illicit that information from them if the coaching relationship is going to continue and flourish.

Support and challenge

Striking the right balance between support and challenge is critical to good coaching. Taken in conjunction with the feedback notes you've just read, *support* represents the occasions when you are reinforcing positive behaviours, especially in areas where the person being coached may still be feeling insecure. 'Despite your nerves, you handled that presentation really well and it'll get easier the more of them you do.'

Challenge, on the other hand, holds up a mirror to negative behaviours to illustrate the impact they may be having. 'Clamming up like you did in the last meeting leaves you feeling frustrated, but it also means that other people think you've got nothing to contribute to the debate, or worse still that you agree with them when you don't.'

Take a look at the support and challenge matrix (Figure 7.1) and see how too much or too little of either of these tools can affect the success of your coaching.

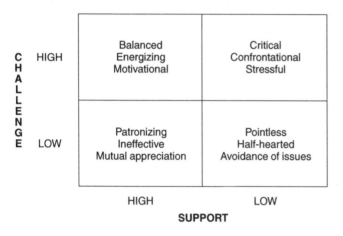

Figure 7.1 matrix content:

		HIGH SUPPORT	LOW SUPPORT
CHALLENGE	**HIGH**	Balanced Energizing Motivational	Critical Confrontational Stressful
	LOW	Patronizing Ineffective Mutual appreciation	Pointless Half-hearted Avoidance of issues

Figure 7.1 The support and challenge matrix

As you can see, where support and challenge are both low (bottom right), the coaching seems pointless and half-hearted. You need to rethink the purpose of the exercise and go back to the basics of objective setting.

The bottom left quarter shows too much support in relation to challenge which turns into an 'ego-massaging' exercise. If everything really were this perfect, why would you bother with coaching at all?

Being over-critical with insufficient praise is a result of the top right box and the exercise can end up degenerating into a 'confrontational' mess. This is the quarter where most bullying bosses are operating.

Finally, having high levels of both support and challenge (top left), in an atmosphere of trust and a commitment to achieving improvements, is a highly energizing experience (often as much as for the coach as the coached). Keep this outcome at the front of your mind when you are coaching.

Because good coaching is about honesty and openness there's no harm in sharing this diagram with your protégé from time to time and talking between yourselves about where you believe the balance is between support and challenge. When people are determined to improve their performance, they're often much harder on themselves than outsiders and you may find that a higher degree of challenge is requested for the future. In this way you can start to accelerate learning.

Tactics

- To be a good coach you need knowledge, engagement, empathy and modesty.
- Coaching means helping people find their own solutions.
- Plan your sessions in conjunction with the person being coached.
- Questioning techniques can help to uncover feelings as well as facts.
- Active listening and an understanding of body language are great assets for coaches.
- The right blend of support and challenge is needed for coaching to be effective.

I can see the carrot at the end of the tunnel. (Stuart Pearce – former England defender)

8

Management

Sound Bite

'In other words, getting the buggers to do what you want, when you want and how you want.'

Managing people is one of the most complex and difficult tasks you will ever encounter; at times it is thankless, tedious and frustrating. Alternatively it can be uplifting, rewarding and the source of great satisfaction; getting it wrong causes you sleepless nights, but the good days are hard to better.

One of the things that makes 'management' so complex is that there is often lots of crossover in the roles and responsibilities of the manager, according to the club/company you work for, some of which you will have seen in previous chapters.

Where the management role really differs from any other is in having to see the big picture of what is going on and needing to take decisions, sometimes with conflicting influences at play, which are designed to have an overall positive effect on the fortunes of the employing organization.

Pundit

Premiership manager and assistant to the England Head Coach, Steve McLaren has had to make the leap from 'number two' to 'number one'. This is how he summed up the difference between the roles:

The biggest difference between being a number one and a number two is decision making – you have a thousand decisions to make in a day as a number one, whereas as a number two you can give a thousand opinions on what should be the right thing, or the right decision to make – as a number one sat in the seat, you have to make that decision.

The following section looks at some of the big things that managers have to cope with, what the role entails and some of the limiting factors that you have to 'manage within'.

Strategy – just what is it?

This is the most overused word in business and it seems to have a different interpretation each time it's spoken. Our view of 'strategy' is that it is nothing more or less complicated than a *plan*, a plan that has three key elements, 'objectives', 'resources' and 'constraints'. The clever thing about a good strategy is that it balances all three of those factors to come up with the optimum outcome.

However, if you keep a cool head and are brave enough to make your strategy simple, you won't go far wrong. Try to make sure that the context of your organization's strategy is right, so the plan should be set in a *realistic* framework that makes it deliverable. All too often people at the head of an organization want to shift the strategic direction by an unrealistic amount, so the CEO of the Fifty Pence chain suddenly declares that they're taking a massive shift upmarket – Oops! I don't think so.

It's not that this kind of change is impossible, but if you've found your niche and it works for you, why change it?

Balance all of this with common sense; if the market moves on drastically, you can't survive with 'ostrich management' – a number of high-profile UK high street chains have suffered this fate in recent years, so you have to keep up with the times.

On the Ball

Keeping up with the times

If you're of 'a certain age', you'll remember the comic strip character Alf Tupper, nicknamed 'the tough of the track'. Each week, Alf would pit his athletic ability against a bunch of toffs and against all odds he would ceaselessly triumph. This gritty Northern character was aided in his endeavours by a diet of fish and chips, which often he'd devour only minutes before racing.

The comic strip was written in the post-war era, when little attention was paid to diet and nutrition; people were just happy that there was enough food to eat. However, had Alf been real and playing football in the modern age, it would be laughable that such an important part of his physiology would not attract close scrutiny from the club he played for.

Premiership clubs now employ full-time staff to assist players with nutrition advice as part of an overall move towards greater professional athleticism. If you don't move with the times, you simply get left behind.

Objectives

Objectives are like oxygen, we need them to survive; they give us a target to aim at, we learn what works and what doesn't, and in the ongoing process of setting objectives we discover the tactics that are effective and successful.

Very often we are part of a hierarchy of objective setting, not all of which we have control over, so in a football environment the owners and directors of the club may have set an objective to finish in the top half of the table; at manager level you have to accept this and find a way of achieving it. Similarly in business you may be handed the top-level objectives of the organization and charged with the task of achieving them.

Your role as a manager is to break the big objective down into more manageable pieces and come to some decisions about how to achieve them. You can only start to do this when you've made an assessment of the other two factors below.

Resources

Fortunately, you will usually have at your disposal a set of resources with which to achieve your objectives, the most useful, though ironically the most expensive, of which is the people around you. Understanding the strengths and weaknesses of each individual will help you to allocate tasks in the most appropriate way, so that your human resources are optimized.

Right at the beginning of this chapter we talked about some of the difficulties of management and the reason is that people are individuals – they all come with their own idiosyncratic set of ideals, hopes, aspirations and 'baggage' from the past. Think about how that affects some of the key elements of management, like recruitment and retention, motivation and disciplinary procedures, and you start to get an idea of what you're up against. Your staff need your attention, often on a one-to-one basis; they want to feel valued, and some even demand nurture.

Beyond the human factor you will need to consider the fixed assets around you, the budget allocations and the variable factors you have control over, like cost management or revenue generation.

Constraints

Sadly, we can't always get what we want and some key resources may be limited, for example money. You may want to buy a new striker or launch a large advertising campaign – indeed, you might see it as critical to the success of the club/company – but if the funds aren't available, your skill will be to make the best of what you've got.

Football fans always admire (though sometimes grudgingly) managers who spend wisely and take their teams to the top flight, but the people they are truly in awe of are those rare managers who, without the benefit of sacks of cash, can take an ordinary-looking team and achieve something great with them, like promotion to the Premiership or an extended Cup run. Wouldn't it be great if every fourth year the Premiership title were awarded to the 'most improved' side?

One of the 'knock-on' effects of having a limited budget is that many managers view it as a case of 'use it or lose it'; any underspend which looks like occurring as year end approaches is suddenly miraculously used up in the kind of spending spree you normally only associate with the January sales. Although it is not necessarily bad, if you spend everything allocated to a particular budget line, this last-minute rush is usually down to bad planning and the upshot can be that money does not get spent wisely (a bit like in the January sales).

Management – a bit like captaincy

In our chapter on captaincy, we talked about how the role could end up as a midpoint between different camps which would sometimes make it difficult to arbitrate. Management is similar to this in some ways, but involves even more multitasking and greater conflicts of interest.

As a football manager you're caught between the board who want success, partly for reasons of glory but more usually to fulfil a financial imperative, the players who have a complex set of objectives, mostly driven by the will to play their best football but complicated by the availability of lots of money, and the supporters, all of whom think they could do a better job.

In fact football clubs often have a mixed relationship with their fan base; on the one hand, these are the people whose hard-earned cash keeps the organization afloat, on the other, this financial support leaves them feeling as though they 'own' a bit of the club. As a 'customer' base you can't question their loyalty, but that has a downside too.

Pundit

Keith Edelman is managing director of Arsenal FC, but has a background in retailing:

I think retail organizations would die to have the kind of relationship with their customers as we have with our fans, but I think that they might find when they'd got it they might wonder about it. So, for example, if you increased the ticket price at Arsenal, which you could probably sell five times over, people wouldn't like it and they'd write in and complain, but they would still pay up. In retail there's a much less intimate relationship, so people are less likely to complain because they know they have free choice to go elsewhere; in a football environment they don't, their loyalty binds them to the club.

Managing in any business other than football has to be easier than that!

Leadership and management

There's an awful lot of crap talked about the difference between leadership and management; yes, they do imply different things, but in any decent organization, or individual within it, you'll find both of them.

Our view is that *leadership is about vision* and *management is about process*; both are equally important if you're going to survive.

Leaders can see where the organization needs to be, they can enthuse others, show the way forward by example, encourage and cajole their troops and make their own passion an infectious thing that pervades everyone around them. Managers understand the steps that have to be taken to get where they want to be; they're good at resource allocation, keeping on top of detail, marshalling people and getting them all heading the same way and overcoming adversity, by a combination of determination, experience and the will to win.

OK, some bosses will be more 'gung-ho' in their approach and others a bit more measured, but it's hard to think of any successful person who hasn't got a fair amount of both these qualities. People with the title of manager will need some leadership qualities in their armoury if they are going to survive, just as those individuals who are seen as leading organizations will have to have management skills (both their own and those of their team) to help realize the vision.

A final word on leadership: it takes bravery, because being a good leader means standing up for what you believe in; there may be times when this might endear you to your own staff, but it can sometimes make you less than popular with your boss.

Politics

This is probably an opportune moment to mention politics, the over-arching term for the power games people play in business. It's very easy to say you're not going to get involved in all that, but much harder to do, especially if the organizational culture supports the doing of deals behind closed doors. Our only advice is on the really important things: stay as honest and true to yourself as you possibly can, don't be afraid to raise sensitive issues amongst peers who are playing games, and in the face of adversity, when it looks like you're being out-manoeuvred, remember that short-term political gain is no substitute for long-term individual integrity. It was Plutonius who said 'if I keep my character, I'll be rich enough'.

On the Ball

A senior manager at a large broadcasting organization would deliberately, maliciously and consistently cloud the issue of reporting lines, ie who was responsible to whom, in order to build her own empire. In meetings with management peers, she would sidestep the issue or, when pressed, give an ambiguous answer. Afterwards she behaved as if the staff in question really did report to her. When one of them stood up to her and asked if it wouldn't be better to clarify the issue she replied 'why on earth would I want to do that, it might undermine *my* position!'

The time and effort spent on this kind of political behaviour is energy sapping and pointless; much better instead to put your efforts into satisfying customers or encouraging staff.

People management

You could fill an entire library with books on people management but it's often made more complicated than it needs to be. Great managers not only possess the ability to be 'process driven', but when it comes to their interaction with people they display the most human of qualities, which include 'compassion', 'concern', 'thoughtfulness' and 'consideration'; in short, they *care*.

Pundit

Derek Hatton is a former Labour politician and lifelong football supporter; he thinks you need to be able to display a range of emotions towards players:

What people don't realize about Alex Ferguson is that whilst he's a very tough disciplinarian, he's the best in the world at putting his arm round a player and I think that is absolutely crucial, in any walk of life; when you're working with people in any sort of way you've got to know when to shout, you've got to know when to be upset, you've got to know when to be angry but you've got to know when to kiss them.

What's the job?

If you take any job description, you can break it down into a series of tasks and responsibilities, which can be flexible according to the individual employed, and the task that has to be achieved. The more someone is able to do, the more you should give them to do, otherwise they'll get bored, stagnate and stop being as efficient over the tasks that are so far within their current ability.

Some key elements that earn you respect and make people feel valued:

■ When you're in a one-to-one meeting, make eye contact.
■ Treat your staff with respect – you reap what you sow.
■ Listen, listen, listen, oh and then listen some more.
■ Lead by example – don't do things you disapprove of in others.
■ Give people your time and attention.
■ Make sure you care – then show them you do.

Get those things right and you'll have cracked some of the toughest challenges of being a manager. Along the way there are pitfalls though, so we've raised some of the side issues you will face below, as being aware of them might help stop your best efforts getting derailed.

Fairness

One of the principal reasons that people fall out with their boss is because they perceive they are being treated unfairly in comparison to their colleagues. In fact, this is one of the central planks of most cases that go to an industrial tribunal; what precedent is there to determine the expectation of the wronged party, and has the employer used the same criteria for judging them as they would for any other employee in a similar or parallel role?

Being discriminatory across a range of areas is now illegal (hence the need for tribunals) and the number of grounds for discrimination is likely to increase in the future. Apart from the fact that you may be breaking the law, it is also bad management practice. Don't be fooled into thinking it only affects the person who is the 'victim'; others who are close by will also see what's going on and though they may choose not to get involved in the conflict, they will judge you none the less.

Getting too friendly

The hardest thing to achieve when you're managing people is to get the relationship with them right. In a 'healthy organization' you will most likely get on well with the people you manage, otherwise how would you be able to maximize your potential and theirs? But you can end up getting on too well.

Some bosses like the idea of socializing with their staff, it's all part of 'team bonding', but others are less keen, feeling that some kind of distance makes for a better working relationship. That's not to say you should be aloof, and if the team invite you to the pub after work on Friday, it might be considered churlish to turn them down. For all that, you need to know your place and if they intend to make a night of it, there's a time for you to dip out, before you either spoil their fun or make a fool of yourself.

Pundit

Here's Steve McLaren's view again:

As coach you're in the dressing room, you're having a cup of tea with them and you join in all the craic and the laugh; as a manager you can't do that – to a certain extent you have to distance yourself. The most difficult part of the job, I suppose, is going through the transition: stepping away from the players and having that distance and just not having the closeness with them and the craic on the field that you used to have; you're looked at differently and you have to act differently.

At the start of this chapter we talked about the conflicting pressures on managers, the need to balance a variety of factors, some of which are directly at odds with others, so imagine you've been out with the team and have become their best friend, only to find on Monday morning that due to cost pressures you're going to have to make 20 per cent of them redundant.

Now, we're not suggesting for a moment that this is an easy task even if you haven't been chummy with them, but the perceived hypocrisy of being best mates one minute and getting rid of them the next is going to make the task of managing those left behind impossible. It's also likely to give you sleepless nights. Management can be lonely, but better that than two faced.

And if one expert view isn't enough for you, here's another, from ex-England captain Bryan Robson.

Pundit

You can't really be friends with the players; I think sometimes that people go overboard and start to be nasty towards their players or are a little bit disrespectful.

I think what you're looking for is a good working relationship where they respect you and you respect them and you get the best out of each other.

More than just friends

A large percentage of long-term relationships and marriages start in the workplace, which is not surprising when you consider that people who have to get along for business reasons are thrown together for 8 to 12 hours every day.

It would be naive to suggest that you should under all circumstances avoid any kind of relationship with a work colleague; however, if you are going to conduct your management responsibilities in a professional way, it doesn't do to have a fling with one of your staff, no matter how attractive the prospect may be.

If it were to work out in the long term, it would be impossible to carry on managing them without cries of favouritism from fellow workers, and if it all falls apart, you've got the added difficulty of having to deal with the fallout!

Motivation

Boss: Okay, your target is going up 20 per cent and lunchtimes have been cut to 15 minutes.
Employee: So what's my motivation here?
Boss: You get to keep your job!

There does still exist in some workplaces a very macho, aggressive and frankly unenlightened school of management, where you attempt to get more work out of people by being horrible to them and scaring them into submission; it's management by fear. However, there's a difference between getting the *most* out of people and the *best* out of them, and even in the case of the former, the bullying tactics won't have much lasting effect.

At the other end of the spectrum is the super-nice boss, who's just seen as a pushover by everyone. 'Damn it, if he can't stand up to us (as employees), how can he ever stand up to the board?' Although it's nice at first to be managed by a 'nice boss', some people soon lose respect for them, become demotivated and start trying to get away with doing as little as possible.

The balance is in the middle, being clear about the task in hand, making it plain what is expected of each member of the team, outlining unequivocally what the rewards will be and monitoring progress along the way.

The final part of the process is designed to keep you informed about what is going on, so that you can make adjustments if it looks like things are going off course. It's broadly what we would define as 'performance management', allowing you to put a halt to behaviours which are damaging the team or the task and encouraging the positive ones, thus motivating the individuals who work for you.

We don't intend to be too gloomy about the job of the manager, but sometimes it is just as well to know what you're up against, and some of the perils we've listed above are commonplace in many walks of business life. When it comes to the practicalities of the job, there's a simple formula for getting people to do the tasks they're allocated and sometimes handling the fallout if they don't do them. In most situations, positive reinforcement is much better than taking disciplinary measures; prevention is better than cure. Coming up is a task allocation system to get things started; it's designed to help you plan your own time as a manager and maximize the potential of your team. This is followed by a section on how to handle conflict if things aren't going as planned.

Training Tip

The twenty list system of task allocation

No matter how hard we try, we never seem to get to the bottom of the 'in tray', and it always seems to be the same tasks that are left incomplete. There are lots of very good reasons for this, not least the fact that work always expands to fill the time available, but it can be frustrating and exhausting if you always have a pile of tasks you wish you'd achieved. When you're managing other people the problem is just as bad for them, but you carry some of the burden of the things they haven't done.

The following system is a good short-term solution to this problem, if you're prepared to commit to it for three months. The starting point is that you list all the tasks you have to do, and we mean all! Everything you've been meaning to get round to, right down to tidying up the office and clearing out your e-mail inbox, gets put on the list. Be as specific as you can and try to break bigger projects down into more manageable chunks; in fact, an hour at a time is a good way of splitting them up.

Keep hold of this master list, as you'll need to refer back to it later, but for now you need to pick 20 things that you intend to achieve in the next 20 working days, that's one a day for a working month.

It's OK to include your day-to-day tasks, but don't fill the list with a single project, broken into 20 units, or the 'in tray' will never get any smaller. It's also important that you have a mix of different things, some of which require your full attention and most concentrated problem-solving abilities and some which you can switch your brain 'off' for.

How you tackle your twenty list is up to you, but it makes sense to spread it out. Balance this with the fact that stretching targets are good and will give you a greater sense of achievement, so consider pushing to get all 20 done in less than the 20 days you've allocated.

There's a great sense of satisfaction in being able to cross things off the list, particularly if they're the tasks you hate or normally never get round to; there's also the added benefit of being able to objectively assess what's important and what's not.

At the end of each week you refer back to your twenty list to see what's been done and you then have the opportunity to re-target yourself for the coming week. A month-end review is essential both to check progress and to set objectives for the following period.

You can carry tasks over from one month to the next, but try to make them higher priority, or you'll come to the end of the quarter with them still left undone. If at the end of the three-month period, you refer back to your master list and find items that never turned up on any of your twenty lists, you've probably established, beyond reasonable doubt, that they're simply not that important, so you should stop worrying about them.

As a manager this is an ideal way of allocating your time, but it's even more useful if you get the rest of the team to do it as well. The important thing here is that you let people set their own tasks, rather than impose your views on them.

Most people instinctively know what they should be doing and they probably feel the same frustration as you at not getting everything finished, so there needn't be any problem in introducing the system.

You can set aside a quick 10 minutes at the end of the week to check on how each team member is doing, which gives you an opportunity to keep them motivated by *praising* them for what's been achieved and urging them on to greater heights in the following week.

We started by saying that this was a three-month exercise, and though you may be tempted to extend it further, it works best as a short sharp shock tactic. There's no harm in resting the idea for a few months and then reintroducing it with a fresh set of objectives. If it becomes part of the everyday work schedule, it will be consigned to the bottom of the 'in tray' – and we already know that nobody ever gets that far down!

When everyone is working hard on completing the tasks on their list, you should find that productivity is running at a high level, but what if one of the team is letting the side down?

Handling conflict

Mostly we've looked at the positive elements of performance in this chapter, but in real life it's not always like that and you will inevitably come into some form of conflict situation with your staff at some stage. In these circumstances, it's worth referring back to our notes on 'discipline' for guidance on how to handle this. Further help comes in the form of a ready-reckoner, called the seven A's of performance management:

- Anger – has no place in handling conflict effectively; wait until you and the other party have calmed down.
- Audience – it's never a good idea to have one; take your one-to-one conflicts behind closed doors, for everybody's benefit. Openly criticizing one employee in front of their colleagues isn't management, it's ritual humiliation.
- Assertiveness – work out carefully what you want to say; if necessary put some bullet points on a Post-it Note and don't shy away from the issues – if something made you angry or upset, don't be afraid of saying so.
- Authority – remember, you are the boss and you have every right to take the issue on. As long as you're fair minded and even handed there can be no criticism of your actions.
- Affirm – state the facts of what has happened as the starting point of any discussion and stick with them; they are the one thing not open to question.
- Avoid – personal criticism of the individual; this is about the actions and behaviours they have indulged in, not how short, thick, fat or ugly they are.
- Accommodate – make sure they have an opportunity to justify or describe the reasoning behind their behaviour, but don't take a long list of excuses as a reason for letting them off for what they've done.

Conducting disciplinary meetings

We've said it before, but it'll stand repetition – shut up and listen! Once you've stated the reason for the meeting and outlined your areas of concern, unless you've got a prima facie case, with unequivocal evidence, at least give the other party an opportunity to describe the situation from *their* point of view.

If you're faced with a situation where you suspect foul play of some kind, then it's time to don the wig and turn into a barrister (though less pompous, obviously!).

In courtroom situations you'll see legal representatives use a technique that starts with a statement of FACTS as they are known; from here they will often form a HYPOTHESIS of the likely outcome from these facts and call upon the witness to CORROBORATE/DENY the allegations.

Now, although you're not in court, this is a useful technique, as long as you remember the importance of applying it with some subtlety. You won't get away with the following: 'Nina, some money has gone missing; you're the one who's always complaining that you're hard up, so I put it to you that you've stolen it.'

On the other hand, this is probably OK: 'Hannah, I was already aware that Andy had upset the customer, but by copying the rest of the team in when you e-mailed me about the situation, it makes it look like you were deliberately trying to undermine him.'

So you start with: 'The facts as we know them are a, b, c.' Follow up with: 'Which leads me to speculate x, y and z.' Then ask: 'But before I make up my mind, I want to hear what you think.'

If you really loathe the thought of this type of meeting, then it's better to avoid it by putting in good management practices in the first place. If everyone knows what's expected of them from the start, you won't have to face conflict nearly as often.

Managers come in all shapes, sizes and flavours; there is no single model for success. You must decide for yourself how to behave, but to give you food for thought, we've contrasted the styles of two of the Premiership's most successful managers.

Earlier in the chapter we heard Derek Hatton's view of Sir Alex Ferguson, widely recognized as one of the greatest club managers of the modern day. He has a reputation for being uncompromising, but at the same time he's protective, almost fatherly to the players in his charge.

Much has been made of the difference between this acerbic Scot and his rival at Arsenal, Arsene Wenger, a man much less disposed to outbursts of emotion (although the rivalry has been stoked up by the tabloid press who know the story will sell papers). It seems that both men have a gift for being able to motivate players, but below we look at the contrast in their styles through a range of players and experts who have had personal contact with them.

Pundit

On Sir Alex Ferguson:

I think the club's a reflection of Sir Alex because the most important man at a club is obviously the manager; everything comes from them. (Mark Hughes)

We were getting beaten at Wimbledon and I experienced it for the first time; Alex, he does mean it, because he was knocking tea cups all over the place. It was true, he was knocking things all over the dressing room, but the thing with Alex is that he says 'I'll test the character and if they're weak, I don't want them in my club – I need strong characters in my club.' (Bryan Robson)

He buys the right type of players, he buys players that can handle being Manchester United players, because it's a difficult environment for a professional footballer if you're not mentally strong. (Mark Hughes)

He was very, very good at getting the best out his players. I think that remains true now when you look at the young players that he's brought on and the discipline that they've been brought up with, and that's his influence. (Mark McGhee)

I have phenomenal admiration for his ability to start again the next season having won it, and to go again, so he's got great enthusiasm – he makes sure the players have it and they're only some of his smaller qualities. Of all the great, great managers, his record in modern-day football is unsurpassed, it's really fantastic. (Martin O'Neill)

On Arsene Wenger:

What I do know is that he raised the standard, there's no doubt about that; he has presented himself in a terrific manner inasmuch as his persona, his attitude, his demeanour, his calmness; all those very good virtues he has in abundance. (John Barnwell)

When Arsene came in there was a lot of worry in the Arsenal dressing room about what training was going to be like, where somebody was going to come in with all these continental ideas and ruin Arsenal football club, but Arsene was very, very clever and within a week he'd won the lads over anyhow because his training was exceptional. (David Platt)

He obviously has a very clear mind of what he wants to achieve, he is extremely fervent in the way he does it, he is not the old-fashioned manager of fists clenched and grit your teeth and coming over the wall with your bayonet fixed, he's a sophisticated man and he is the archetypal modern manager. (John Barnwell)

Very, very studious, very approachable and has his own ideas of the game; very strong minded, but he didn't raise his voice really; he gained

*the respect of the players very, very quickly because of what he did on the
training pitch. (David Platt)*

It's not for us to conclude whether one style is better than the other; what is
more important is to recognize is that both men are true to their characters,
they conduct their business in the best way they know how, each has a
passion for the game (although it manifests itself in different ways) and
their determination has brought success to both clubs.

It just goes to show that there's more than one way of achieving the end
of becoming a successful manager.

Tactics

- ▦ Managing people is difficult, but it can be equally rewarding.
- ▦ Think of strategy as a simple, deliverable plan.
- ▦ Remember the importance of objectives, resources and constraints.
- ▦ Leadership is about vision, management is about process.
- ▦ Politics are part of everyday management life, but can be time
  consuming and unproductive.
- ▦ Treat your people with fairness and they'll repay you with commitment.
- ▦ Managers often need to stay one step removed from their staff; it
  doesn't pay to get too friendly.
- ▦ If you have to handle a disciplinary situation, plan what you are going
  to say and act with sensitivity.

Q. Who is your closest friend at the club?
A. (Gordon Strachan) I am the manager, I have no friends.

Selection

'Picking the best team for the job is critical to success, but there are so many variable factors.'

If you disassemble the structure of a football club or a business, underneath the fixed assets, the tangibles and intangibles, the goodwill, beneath everything else, you'll be left with the people.

The thing that drives success or courts failure is the human condition. This presents a problem, not least because as individuals we're simply too complex to define in any systematic, scientific, manageable way; there are too many character traits, too many combinations to make sense of. Even when put into groups, the best we can do is spot general trends, overarching moods or vague tendencies. No wonder team selection is so difficult.

Before you even think about picking your best team, you have to assemble a talent pool from which to select and that's where the hard work begins.

The difference here between football and business is the number of people involved. Football allows for only a very few individuals to make it on the professional stage and there are clear lines of definition which surround this, not least the fact that at any one time you're allowed a maximum of 11 players on the pitch. This has the advantage of making the issue much more specific than in the commercial world, where only at the top level do you find headhunters looking for specific skills to fill particular roles. There are still many similarities in the way the two disciplines handle their search for, and selection of, talent.

Supply and demand

This fundamental law of economics has a dramatic effect on the price we have to pay for anything, and talent is no exception. When demand is greater than supply it means that what you're looking for is sought after by many people, and as a consequence the price goes up. This holds true just as much for a personnel director as a proven striker.

When the balance is the other way around (ie supply exceeds demand), you are effectively in a 'buyer's market', where the power lies with the purchaser. There are now tons of similarly skilled people about and the buyer can pick and choose who they want, the result being that the price falls.

What has caused hyperinflation in some sectors is the realization that the talents required are of an extremely rare and skilled variety, that very few individuals possess them and that they attract an 'audience' simply because of their rarity value. This has happened increasingly in recent years in show business, particularly film and television, where the addition of a star name can add several noughts to the box office takings or tens of thousands to the ratings. In this context, it is known as 'artist inflation', and has become a major 'cost element' in any production. In football, the same phenomenon has occurred, where in some circles it is known as 'absolute madness'.

Although most of us in business don't often witness this in our company, you do see at the top level deals done with specific company directors that can run into millions of pounds, though increasingly there is pressure to link these closely to the *performance* of the organization as a whole. Because the most significant cost of running a business is the people, market conditions at any one time can have a dramatic effect on the level of investment required.

Superstars may be rare in business, but it's still true that the laws of supply and demand apply throughout the various tiers within the company, so when the nation as a whole has very low levels of unemployment, the cost of labour rises. What we can also learn from football is that the higher the skill level, the rarer it is, so if you're looking for a specific set of qualifications and experience in any post you're trying to fill, it will be harder to find and therefore more costly on a pro rata basis than lower down the skills spectrum.

The squad approach

In order to be able to field a team every week, football clubs need a pool of people, greater in number than 11, to choose from. This has brought about the formation of squads, with a recognition that the demands of the game at the top flight are so great that sometimes more than one team is needed. The 'rotation system' has become popular, giving players the chance to 'have a game off' and rest, in order that they'll be at the peak of fitness for the next match they play.

As a business manager, this might seem like a difficult concept to apply to the 'squad' in your charge, but subconsciously it's happening all the time. If you value the contribution of your 'top performers', and you know they've been working flat out to hit a deadline or complete a project, you should naturally encourage them to take their foot off the gas once it's all over, although in our experience many senior managers don't appreciate the importance of metaphorically 'having a game off'.

Great managers go a step further in this recognition and verbalize their feelings to their staff, praising them for their efforts and 'rewarding' them with an overt offer of greater leeway on start and finish times, for example. This 'resting' of talent isn't as obvious as in the world of soccer, but it should happen more than it does.

Getting the right team

There are lots of factors to consider when you're putting together a winning team and they're not all to do with personalities.

Pundit

Ex-England boss Graham Taylor thinks that it's the combination of individual players working together that is critical to good selection: 'I think the team is the all-abiding thing, even allowing for having great individual players within that team; you want them to express themselves but the team becomes the most important thing.'

Structure

If you've got a blank sheet of paper and are required to put a team together, the starting point is to assess the job in hand and draw up a structure. You can only do this if you have a firm idea of the 'formation' you want to play. So you begin by deciding which roles are necessary, and then defining the skills needed to fill them.

The roles in a newly formed sales team would include front-line sales people, admin staff, support staff and management; this would be very different to setting up a production plant, with shop floor staff, team leaders, logistics managers and admin. Indeed, the approach you take in team selection will be directly linked to the objective you need to achieve.

Gap identification

Once you've got a clear idea of the roles within the team, based on your knowledge of the individuals concerned, you can then start to put names against them. What usually happens in these situations is that the first few are easy; every 'player' aspires to be the first name on the team sheet and managers know who their top performers are, so the matching process is simple.

Things get more difficult when there's not a natural choice for a specific role, and what starts to appear is a 'skills gap'. Depending on what world you're operating in, this could either be 'insufficient height at the back' or 'inadequate knowledge of relevant software packages'; either way, identifying the problem is part of the process of starting to solve it.

Solution 1 – more training

With a clear idea of where the weaknesses lie in the team, a possible solution, at least for the medium term, is to embark on a programme of relevant training with the most appropriate members of the squad. Here you have to weigh natural ability with the propensity to learn. You're striking a balance between the inborn traits of the individual (tall, athletic, well coordinated or clever, articulate, capable) and the skills that can be taught (ball control, awareness or IT literacy, marketing experience).

Experience teaches us when to invest in training and when it's better to get a better-matched individual in, but if you sometimes forget that you have a choice, then remember what we said at the start of Chapter 1: 'You can teach a turkey to climb a tree, but it's better to hire a monkey.'

Solution 2 – the search for talent

If you've exhausted yourself with turkey-training to no avail, it's maybe time to move on and find yourself a monkey.

Before you start the search, you need a clear definition of the 'must haves' and a shopping list of additional 'nice to haves'. In the first category, it's essential to include the skills which will fill your gap or shortage, or else you'll end up with another turkey. At the same time, however, it's worth considering the other skills in the team to see if you can supplement them. A good solid right back, who is also pretty handy in goal, might just come to your rescue one day. In the same way, a sales professional with a fair command of copy-writing skills may just prove to be the asset you're looking for.

Attracting talent

Sad to say, the biggest pull for any talent is money; as they say, everyone has their price. At the top level of the 'beautiful game' there is the added complication that all players now have agents and they have a living to make too. It's hard not to be drawn to the highest bidder. There have been a few notable exceptions in the Premiership, where players have turned down the best financial offer because they have felt 'loyal to the club' they've been with since they turned professional, but we're being careful not to name them in case they've buckled under the weight of the money by the time you read this!

However, if you're a club or business that hasn't got a bottomless pit of money, what can you do to make yourself more attractive? For the answer to this you have to ask what it is that people value from their employment aside from money, and it's very often described in terms of things like 'reputation', 'integrity', 'image' and 'track record'.

Among top employers there has been more and more talk about the 'employer brand' versus the 'consumer brand'. That's to say, you might expect an organization like Microsoft to be young, trendy and techy in its approach and you'd be disappointed if you went to work there and found something different inside the organization (incidentally, you won't!).

So there needs to be consistency in what you look like from the outside, to what you offer employees on the inside. Media organizations struggle more than most with this as by the nature of their business, they have a 'superficial glamour' attached to them. Ask anyone who works in the media if the glamour is real and they'll tell you 'no'.

If you want further evidence, try to get a look at a 'real life' television studio; a 'set' which appears big and glossy when we watch from our armchair can often look small and shabby close up. An established and respected set designer once said, 'I rue the day that colour television was invented; before that you could paint the flats (the large backdrop scenery) any colour you wanted; it all looked grey to the viewers!'

The challenge to business now is that we have to 'live the image'; if you present yourself to the world as an organization with high ethical standards, you'd better make sure you're living them or your new recruits will soon become disillusioned and cynical.

While we're on the subject of attracting the best people, we need to bear in mind that it is often a mix of different types blended together that makes the best team. This is most definitely the case in top-level football, where teams are increasingly made up of players from all over the world. Some businesses have been slow to follow this model, though now it is a matter of law as well as ethics.

Diversity and discrimination

These two words are often linked together in a business context, but their juxtaposition is interesting because of the connotations of each; *diversity* is a positive word encapsulating all that's good about having a rich and varied mixture; *discrimination*, on the other hand, is filled with negative nuances that suggest a narrow-mindedness and meanness of spirit.

Possibly the highest-profile anti-racism campaign the UK has ever seen has come from the world of football, where, except in a few rare circumstances, there's an acceptance of people for what they are. Even on the terraces where racism was once rife, there is a much wider acceptance of all players on the basis of their ability, not their ethnic origin.

There are many reasons why diversity is embraced so wholly; it's partly due to recognizing that no single group of people or race has all the right answers, partly down to learning skills from people who have different backgrounds from us, and partly down to the recognition that if we don't look at wider horizons, we'll never see what might have been achievable.

Pointers to good selection

Here are a few things to bear in mind before you embark on team selection; they're designed as a quick reference guide:

■ *Flexibility* – this is desperately important, because you have to be able to adapt your selection to fit a number of criteria beyond your control, including what the opposition/competition are capable of.
■ *Awareness* – selection can't happen in a vacuum, you have to take account of the environment, of what's going on around you. Just as some players are better in certain circumstances (eg they may be able to rise to the big occasion better than others), so in business you might need to select the best 'team' for a particular meeting or project or client. Sometimes in the world of advertising you will find a creative genius with an ability to come up with winning ideas, but put them in front of the client and they fall apart.

■ *Resourcefulness* – if things go wrong and your back is to the wall, how good will you be at problem solving? If you suddenly discover your star player is ill, how will you cover the gap that leaves? Making the very best of what is at your disposal (even when it's subject to last-minute change) is the sign of a good manager.

■ *Intuition* – a difficult-to-define quality that sets you apart from the pack. How well can you judge the mood of those around you and make fine adjustments to the way you play the game?

Organic management

There is no textbook that can tell you how you should manage people; yes, you can learn tips and techniques, but the way you apply them is down to your individual style – and it's this that makes one manager different from the next. In this context, it's useful to think of selection as a 'living' thing. You need to change and respond to many different circum-stances if you are to fulfil your potential as a 'selector'.

What might some of those factors be in football?

■ Suspension or injury – do you have all the players you want available?
■ Form – who's playing well or badly?
■ Opposition – who are you trying to beat?
■ Mood – what's morale like in the team?
■ Conditions – like the weather, the state of the pitch.

These can be short-term factors, as the opposing team changes week by week in football; however, even if the timescales are longer in business, the list of factors is just as varied:

■ Competition – beating old adversaries and looking out for new entrants.
■ Economy – is it buoyant or depressed, are you fit to weather any storm?
■ Budget – how much do you have to spend?
■ Politics – what impact do world events have on your ability to compete?
■ Culture – is your organization aggressive or passive, and how does that affect your decisions?

Fitness versus spirit

When we looked at the list of criteria for selecting new talent, we suggested that a 'skills list' be drawn up to match the 'gap' in the team and went on to say that this should include both 'must haves' and 'nice to haves'. Because human beings are complex creatures there are other things to take into account, features that may vary over time according to your skill as a people manager.

When we talk about fitness in this context we're looking at the skills and abilities of the individual. Do they have what it takes to be physically and emotionally able to complete the tasks you're going to set? Are they fit for purpose?

Spirit is about their *willingness* to do what you ask.

Today's leading management thinkers are in agreement that if you could pick only one of these things, you'd choose the latter. If someone has the will, enthusiasm and desire to do the job you've employed them for, even if their skill set isn't an immediate match, then someday, somehow you may be able to train them up. On the other hand, if someone is the best exponent of the skills you're seeking, but they just don't give a damn, you can pour endless energy into getting them 'onside' and never achieve anything.

So if you have two candidates to choose from, look at who's up for the task and you'll make the right selection.

Pundit

Selection is a difficult business made all the harder by the fact that we don't always have the resources we'd like at our disposal. Taking a pragmatic approach and 'managing with what you've got' is the advice from Gary Megson. During a four-year spell at West Bromwich Albion he took the club into the Premiership twice and knows all about managing within limitations:

Management is about doing what you can do, not what you would like to do; there's no point in saying we're going to have 50 passes to try and score a goal if you haven't got anybody in the team who's particularly comfortable on the ball, so I think as regards management you come in with these great ideals of this is how I'm going to get my team to play and this is what I'm going to insist on; your team has got to be capable of doing those things and I think you've got to look at what you've got, have a look at the scope and manage within that.

Get the best out of what you've actually got; even if you have your eye on what you want to bring in, you're a very fortunate person if you can just say 'these are my ideals, I'll go and buy players to fit them'; most of us have to see what we've got and play the best that we can.

Tactics

- The laws of supply and demand alter the price you have to pay for talent.
- Businesses and football teams need to build a talent pool to select from.
- Selection involves finding new people and ensuring that you are training your existing 'squad'.
- Being true to your *values* is essential if you expect to retain the best people in your organization.
- Blending different types of people together often results in fielding the best team.
- People's *willingness to work hard* is often more important than their skills mix.

The FA Cup touches so many people. It's a fair bet that, by the end of today, players you've never heard of will be household names – like that fellow who scored for Sutton United against Coventry City last season. (Bobby Campbell – former Chelsea manager)

10

Opposition

Sound Bite

'This would all be so much easier if other people didn't want to beat us at our own game.'

If football teams have one great advantage over businesses, it is that they always know exactly where they stand in relation to the opposition. A league table charts their position with every match played. The proprietor of a commercial enterprise will have a much vaguer picture of their ranking, but there's still a lot that can be learnt from the 'beautiful game'.

First, though, to clear up an issue of definition: where we use the word 'opposition' in a football context, we're more likely to use 'competition' in business, but they mean much the same thing.

The following analysis is based on how football clubs approach the whole issue of 'opposition', their attitude towards it and the actions they take to try to combat it. As you read through, try to envisage how this would play out in your business and the things you could do differently in future to combat the opposition/competition.

Who are they, where are they?

If you look up over the parapet and can't see your competitors, then they're probably hiding in the long grass stalking you, because unless you're incredibly lucky, it's not very likely that you'll have none.

One of the critical things that all football clubs do is that they identify, define and rank their opposition to get a true picture of who it is critical to beat. Looking at the Premiership from the outside you might be deluded into thinking that all matches carry the same weight (the points system would have you believe that, with a maximum of three at stake in each game), but this is far from the case.

If you were only promoted last season and your objective this year is solely about survival in the top flight, then it's much more important to concentrate your efforts on the clubs who will potentially be fighting off relegation at the end of the season. Every game against one of these clubs is defined as a 'six-pointer', meaning that a victory over them not only adds three points to your tally, but deprives them of the opportunity to do likewise.

Equally, you can alter the aspiration of your team when playing one of the top six clubs; of course you won't go out to lose, but if it does happen, you can content yourself with the fact that it's not as critical a game as against your 'near opposition'.

Not only does this give a clear focus for your efforts, but it also helps with team morale as you can manage the expectation of the squad as you proceed through the fixture list.

It's ridiculous in business to think about taking on the world, when a more narrow focus for your attention is likely to yield better results. Take a small, independent, town centre store as an example and you'll see that the best approach is to try to take as much of the share of all the revenue spent in the locality as possible, rather than try to compete with the out of town hypermarket. Think back to the Toyota mission statement 'Beat Mercedes' as an example of focused thinking.

Weighing up your advantage

When you take a marketing-led approach to doing business, an easy way of finding out how highly you're ranked in the marketplace is to do a SWOT analysis of strengths, weaknesses, opportunities and threats. If you complete this honestly and do the same for your competitors (in as much as you know them), it will provide a pretty accurate picture of where you are now and offer some pointers to the future.

In football, where hard cash seems to play a bigger and bigger part in defining one club's advantage over another, the analysis has to be much more creative. If the super-clubs at the top level can go and buy whichever player they want, it's going to be hard to compete in that arena, but football clubs are made up of many other important ingredients. If you're a cash-strapped club, here are some of the areas you'd probably consider:

- team spirit;
- morale;
- loyalty of your supporters;
- ability to grow talent;
- never-say-die attitude;
- character;
- fitness;
- stamina;
- strength;
- passion;
- ambition;
- determination;
- fairness;
- community spirit;
- leadership;
- camaraderie, and more.

It would be naive to suggest that all this would be any consolation if at the end of the season you are still relegated; even the British will only put up with being 'plucky losers' so often. But football is about more than winning everything at all costs, otherwise why would anyone support a team outside the top half-dozen?

Sometimes you have to be creative in establishing where your competitive advantage is both in football and in business, but with a bit of thought around the outside of the core subject, you can come up with areas where you score higher than any other player in the market.

The added benefit of doing this sort of analysis is that it brings a healthy dose of reality to your thinking, *so instead of setting targets for the business that have been plucked out of the air (at best aspirational, at worst pie-in-the-sky), you can set your objectives in the context of where you really are right now.*

Exploiting your analysis

All of this 'competitor analysis' is going partly to waste if you don't use what you've learnt to your advantage. Knowing that a team is weak on the left side or poor at handling set pieces gives you the opportunity to think in advance about ways you can exploit them. If that 'exploitation' all seems a bit underhand, then consider another sporting analogy, that of the heavyweight boxer. Imagine you're in the ring with someone who has a clear disadvantage in one element of their make-up; are you going to maximize your advantage by concentrating on that area, or are you going to stand there and let him punch you very hard and often, while you consider the moral arguments?

Back to football and things like 'home advantage' spring to mind, along with any injuries or suspensions that might be keeping key players out of the opposing team; alternatively, in business, it could be that a competitor is having supply difficulties or quality issues, which you may pick up from a customer who uses you both. In these situations a degree of caution needs to be exercised over how you exploit the advantage and it's better to point out the solidity of your own supply chain, or your meticulous attention to quality control, rather than be seen to be criticizing their inability to deliver.

One of the key issues here is 'response times' and if you see an opportunity to capitalize on your advantage you need to be flexible enough to implement the strategy right away. If you take too much time to weigh up all the pros and cons, the opportunity may have passed you by.

What are they playing at?

If you are to have any chance of making the most of your competitive advantage you need to know *what it is*, and *how it changes* on a day-to-day basis. This means you need to monitor what's going on with the opposition all the time. Have they bought a new player, changed their training and coaching methods, introduced a new physiotherapist, or employed the services of a sports psychologist? Any, all, or none of these things could make a significant difference to their performance, but if you don't know what's going on, you stand no chance of being able to combat it.

In the fast-moving consumer goods sector, where some companies still employ a large sales force on the ground, each member of the team is required to report back on a monthly basis on competitor activity in their sales territory. This might be the launch of a new product, a price promotion or more shelf space in store. The critical thing is that without the information, there is no way of devising strategies to meet it.

On the Ball

The jealous ostrich

The early 1980s saw a revolution in the drinks industry, brought about not by meticulous research into consumer tastes and inventive product development to meet new desires, but by changes in packaging technology.

Up to that point, the bottled sector of the industry used glass returnable or disposable (recyclable) bottles, but two new innovations came along. First, the Tetra Pak (or Tetra brick as the trade called it, because of its similarity in size and shape to a brick – why else?), and then the PET bottle, the kind of plastic bottle that most soft drinks are still sold in today.

The clever companies embraced the new developments wholeheartedly, but the traditionalists buried their heads in the sand and found fault with the new packaging. 'People will never drink orange juice out of a cardboard carton' or 'these new bottles give the drink a plasticky taste'. History has been the judge of who was right.

Keep your eye on the opposition and plan ahead

Short vs. long vs. reactive

We've already talked about sizing up the opposition and deciding who is the most important, but it's vital to the success of the club (or business) to keep a watch on the longer-term future too. This Saturday's match (this month's sales target) may be preoccupying your thoughts today, but without a bigger picture to set this in context, you may end up always worrying about the short term and never putting in place any strategies to cope with what's happening further down the road.

Planning is the key to success, or at least it's the key to knowing that you didn't quite reach where you wanted to be and that is just as good. At least you had a benchmark in the first place, something to aim for; something to tell your people about and inspire and enthuse them with, to try harder. Without a plan you just drift along not knowing when you're failing and, much more importantly, when you're succeeding, when to celebrate, when to congratulate the team on a job well done. Without those things, how can you possibly hope to motivate people?

Keep in mind the immediate objective, but also look towards the horizon and think what the longer-term future might hold. The final piece of the planning jigsaw is 'contingency planning'. You need to think about 'worst' and 'best' case scenarios that could come up in the next 12 months and decide what you'd do under those special circumstances. By doing this you have an opportunity to be reactive to situations that occur and often it is those who react first who steal the advantage (see the jealous ostrich story).

Some thoughts on 'gap analysis'

If you're trying to beat the opposition, your analysis of where you stand in comparison to them will start to stir your thoughts. However, one of the essential elements of any planning session is to work out not only where you are now, but where you want to be, then you can see the size of the gap between the two points. Only then can you start to understand the task in front of you.

Training Tip

Planning to win

At this stage, it's maybe worth referring back to many of the things we looked at in the 'first half' and charting how much of each you have as an individual and an organization. Think about skills and experience; do you have everything you need in the right place at the right time or is some training or additional recruitment needed? How well does everyone understand the task ahead, and are they ambitious enough to reach for it? What can you do to show your passion and translate your enthusiasm to others so that they'll try even harder? What kinds of stresses and strains will that put on people? Are they fit to cope? Do you have a strategy in place to relieve the pressure from them now and again? Thinking about and planning for these things will put you in a much better position to beat the opposition, in both the short and long term.

Competitive strategies

Your competitive strategy is all about how you play the game. Although as each fixture comes up you might adapt your tactics to try to exploit the weaknesses of the opposition, it's almost certain that you'll have a particular way of playing. This is how teams get reputations as 'boring', 'defensive', or 'exciting'. Both formation and attitude have a role to play, and sometimes it's obvious when a team is merely playing for a draw.

In business, it's more likely that the key planks of competitiveness are going to centre around price and product, so it's vital to know what different approaches will mean.

As more and more products become commoditized, meaning that consumers can go to any number of suppliers and obtain pretty much the same thing, the temptation increases all the time to compete on price; while this might increase demand in the short term and win you some market share points, the difficulty is that this strategy is the least sustainable in the long term. It might be adopted because of a lack of imagination, an unsophisticated marketing approach or a route-one-for-goal attitude to business, but you can guarantee there will always be another competitor in the market who will try to undercut you and steal back the share of customers.

Time and again we see this kind of price war being played out, which is great news for us as consumers, but much less fun if you happen to run one of the organizations that's fighting the war. Most marketing experts will tell you that in a price war, no company wins.

The alternative to this is to compete on 'added value' attributes. That is to say, you increase the number of things that customers value, and do your best to make them an integral part of your offering. Even so, it's hard in many instances to preserve this value for any length of time, as a competitor who sees your product outperforming theirs is soon likely to copy the 'extras' you've built in.

The car market is a great example of this. In the 1970s cars were pretty basic and certainly if you wanted any sophisticated extras (like a radio, for example!) you had to pay extra. To gain a foothold in the UK market, Japanese manufacturers started fitting more and more 'added value' items as standard; this trend has continued to the point where we now have a universal expectation of electric everything, aircon, ABS brakes and those little cup holder things for your can of Coke.

We've also seen increasingly elaborate attempts to add value through image, with advertising that offers us a lifestyle beyond our dreams if only we buy such and such a car. Now you can get performance, economy, an attractive family, a top executive job, and a choice of pretty girls (or boys if you prefer) thrown in. Whatever next? If it were us, we'd consider adding another cup holder.

For all of the difficulties of this, it's still a better strategy in the long term than heading down the cheapest-price route, unless you're 100 per cent convinced that no one, anywhere, is going to be able to reduce their cost base lower than yours, either now or in the future.

A final thought on pricing policy vs the competition. You need to consider the arguments of price vs yield. That is to say, if by cutting your price by 10 per cent you were to double your turnover, how much additional profit would ensue? Of course, it's virtually impossible to say unless you're prepared to test it, but it's food for thought when you're setting your prices.

In the example of the car industry above, you'll see how elements of added value can change over time. Sometimes this can be down to changes in technology, like the addition of satellite navigation systems that simply hadn't been invented back in the 1970s. But technology isn't the only source of newly discovered added value; sometimes economic, political or social factors can have an effect as well. One such case is the increasing emphasis being put on CSR, or corporate social responsibility, to give it its full title.

This started out with what most people considered a few well-meaning loonies introducing 'ethical' trading into their terms of business. Despite the growing tide of consumers who saw this as a valuable addition to the product offering, it was still considered to be outside the mainstream of business.

That was until the crash of huge companies such as WorldCom and Enron because of questionable accounting practices. Suddenly people started to wake up and look at these cases, add them to what they'd heard about exploitation of labour in the Far East and the damage to the environment caused by some global corporations, and the weight of opinion caused a shift in attitude. Since then, many large organizations have installed CSR as a critical element of their trading policy, going so far as to use it as an element of competitive advantage.

Getting the big things right

The problem with business, football and life in general is that we often get dragged down by the detail and mired in the minutiae. In reality, if we concentrate on getting the big things right most of the time, then we won't go far wrong. This theory is backed up by the Pareto principle, a posh name for the 80:20 rule. In many businesses, analysis of turnover will show that 80 per cent of revenue comes from only 20 per cent (in number) of the customers and yet equal time, effort and resources are poured into servicing everyone.

If you could ditch the 80 per cent who are contributing the least and reduce the cost base (servicing costs) accordingly, then the enterprise would be much more profitable. Back in the real world this is difficult to achieve, but what this example should do is signal that you need to spend most of your valuable time and effort on keeping the top 20 per cent happy. In the same way, if you get the 20 per cent of really big things you have to do in a day right, you can pretty much stop worrying about the rest.

In football, if you consistently score more goals than the teams you are playing against, you don't need to concern yourself over the colour of the paint in the dressing rooms.

Tactics

■ Identifying the opposition is the first step to being able to beat them.
■ Take time to understand your own market position; what do you have that is unique?
■ Stick to what you're good at, but keep an eye on what everyone else is doing.
■ Making contingency plans avoids last-minute panics.
■ Competing only on price is usually a recipe for disaster.
■ Try to get the big things right most of the time and don't worry too much about the detail.

The road to ruin is paved with excuses. (Bobby Gould – ex-Coventry City manager)

11

Full time

Sound Bite

'Some people are on the pitch...'

Well, no, it's not all over, not quite yet. Yes, the final whistle has blown and you're busy swapping shirts with the opposing team, but it doesn't end here. Think what professional footballers do once they've left the field, what happens in the aftermath of the match (try your best to keep your thoughts pure).

Professional athletes warm down gently; if they're carrying an injury, they'll often spend some time standing in a wheelie bin full of ice to speed the healing process (no, honestly, they really do). After that they join their teammates and talk about the game. Then, if they've got any sense, they try to forget about it and relax in whatever way they choose.

A few days later they turn up for training again and watch a video of the match, while the manager and coach point out the good bits and the not so good. Then they start all over again preparing for their next outing.

So, in sequence, as a business professional, what do you do when you leave the office, when the final whistle has blown?

First things first; take good care of yourself – we don't necessarily recommend the 'ice bin' but a hot bath might do you the world of good. If you've got a sympathetic partner, you might indulge in a bit of post-match analysis, but try not to bore him or her too much! To keep your work/life balance in kilter, it's good to have plenty of things to do which are not related to your job. Make the most of this time; maybe you've got children who demand your attention – try to give it to them without being distracted by the number of e-mails you've got waiting for you to deal with. Otherwise a visit to the gym, the pub, the cinema or even a night in front of the telly will do you good, as long as you're able to switch off from work.

After you've 'warmed down' or, more appropriately, wound down, resolve to make some time now and again to think about what's gone before, analyse what's working and what isn't, and, just like with the video review process that goes on in football grounds on a regular basis, get your team together to really look at what you're doing. The more inclusive you are, the more likely it is that people will contribute freely to the debate. Although it's pointless to dwell on the past, time set aside in this way can be really valuable for generating new, fresh ideas on how to 'beat the opposition' next time.

In the spirit of this analysis, we've summarized the important points from this book, to give you a ready-reminder of the important elements, both of the 'beautiful game' and for business and management generally.

Be passionate. If you're lucky you already are wholeheartedly committed to what you do. If not, then hopefully you are in a position to change that, either by renegotiating your role and responsibilities with your existing company or by thinking about what does fire you up and finding a new job that will make you happier.

Learn new skills every day. Many professional bodies now incorporate CPD (continuous professional development) as part of their terms of membership and we equally hear much from government bodies about lifelong learning. Apart from anything else, having new challenges is stimulating and can often re-energize you if you're starting to feel jaded about your current role; finding new ways of doing things, or new things to do, can be extremely invigorating. This doesn't have to be directly related to work either; you could choose to go to an evening class at a local college and improve your skills in something you already enjoy. We live in such an interrelated world today, especially when it comes to technology, that even a seemingly non-work skill might prove useful. Aside from anything else, you'll get the chance to meet new people, which as well as providing a stimulus in itself, can make us think seriously about what we do for a living and perhaps re-assess its worth.

If you're still having trouble choosing what to learn, think back to the combination we talked about in Chapter 1: a good skills mix includes the technical, the tactical and the practical; which is the area you need to spend most time on improving?

While you're in this learning mode, don't lose sight of the fact that it's a good idea to play to your strengths. Stick to what you're good at and try to develop in that area, rather than devoting lots of time to things you may never master. If you're creative by nature, then learn something new that's associated with creativity (digital photography perhaps); if, on the other hand, your strength is 'people skills', it might be wiser to get involved with a local charity that's crying out for someone who can marshal a team together and take some action that benefits the community.

None of the extra effort that you put in will be wasted if you have the will to win. Ambition is a great driver and motivator, especially in situations where support from others is low and we need a large degree of self-reliance. A degree of moderation is always wise though; if you find yourself in situations where you're tempted to 'cheat' in order to get on, it's time to take a step back and consider if this is the right role for you.

Remember the importance of speaking a second language. We alluded to this especially in our chapter on captaincy, but it can be really useful in all walks of business life. It's really a shorthand way of saying that *there's huge benefit in being able to see the world from another person's point of view*. If you speak the language of the top floor or shop floor, it is without doubt that you'll be able to learn something new from the people at the other end of the spectrum. In management positions it's a great way of finding out how the business really works, and you might also pick up some vital information if you talk to the people at the customer interface. On the other hand, if you're grafting away with the other workers and wondering what and why you do what you do, it might give you a better understanding if you spend some time with someone from 'upstairs' to get a view of the business as a whole. There is nothing more demotivating than a repetitive role where you're not even sure what you're contributing to the enterprise.

Your 'second language' will come in really handy if you find that you've got to coach someone else. Although we made a number of points about the best way to approach this, if you only take one on board we think the most important is that *coaching is a process whereby you help others to find their own solution to the issues they face, not offer your own 'ready made' answer*. Not only is the learning embedded more deeply, but you will also increase their sense of satisfaction and self-worth if they've had the opportunity to work through the problem, with you as a support.

Deal with people fairly. It's not just the law, it's good business practice. The gripe you most often hear from disaffected workers is that their boss simply isn't fair; they show favouritism, and that kind of behaviour not only harms the 'victims', it also breaks down team spirit, so everyone (not to mention the business itself) suffers.

Select the best possible team you can for the job in hand. If you've got areas of your game that are weaker than others, recognize this fact and make sure that the less experienced members of the squad get plenty of help and support from the older hands. *Praise and encourage them all;* a well-placed word at the right time does a lot more for motivation than the annual haggling over pay increases.

If you find yourself in a situation where it's all gone horribly wrong and there is a need to instigate some kind of disciplinary procedure (which can be anything from a formal warning right down to a 'telling off'), be confident enough to take the issue on, rather than shy away from it. In the end we have to face up to the fact that *conflict is part of business; you can attempt to minimize it through clear communication and good management practices, but if it happens, part of the job is confronting it.* Don't 'flame' people on e-mail, use sarcasm as a way of hinting at your displeasure or bawl them out in front of colleagues. Make time to organize a civilized one-to-one meeting and calmly lay out your case, giving them a right to reply and ensuring that you reach some kind of agreement on what behaviours you expect in the future.

Pundit

As we're now into 'time added' for injuries, a final expert opinion comes from Graham Taylor. Unlike Bill Shankly's famous quote that 'football isn't a matter of life or death, it's more important than that', Taylor's opinion is more balanced, and while this isn't meant to depress you, as you trudge off the field, it's worth remembering his wise words as a way of keeping either football or our working lives in some kind of proportion: 'You must see the big picture and you must always remember that although it's a great game, a marvellous game and we all want to be successful, at the end of the day we all become yesterday's men.'

This leads us to a final thought about what we do for a living and how we do it; our advice is that you should spend some time focusing on you and what you want out of life. Work is now such a big part of what we do, it's often a primary source of our self-worth and happiness; looked at like that, it's too big a thing to get wrong. You need to keep in mind your work/life balance and try to make sure that each element complements the other. In football and in business you reap what you sow; hopefully what we've shared from our own experience and our research will help you find the most fertile soil.

Is that an overweight female soprano I can hear in the background? In that case it really is all over now!

Additional reading

Arnold, J (2005) *Work Psychology*, FT Prentice-Hall, London (see chapters on personnel selection, assessing people at work, motivation)

Blanchard, K and Johnson, S (1983) *The One Minute Manager*, Willow, London

Burke, R and Cooper, C (eds) (2004) *Leading in Turbulent Times*, Blackwell Publishers, Oxford

Cooper, C L (ed) (2004) *Leadership and Management in the 21st Century*, Oxford University Press, Oxford

Lewis, S and Cooper, C (2005) *Work–Life Integration*, John Wiley & Sons, Chichester

Palmer, S *et al* (2003) *Creating a Balance: Managing Stress*, British Library Press, London

Sparrow, P (2003) *The Employment Relationship*, Elsevier, London

Sutherland, V and Cooper, C (1997) *Dealing with Difficult People*, Kogan Page, London

Theobald, T and Cooper, C (2004) *Shut Up and Listen: The Truth About How to Communicate at Work*, Kogan Page, London

Weightman, J (2004) *Managing People*, CIPD Books, London

Index